TUDOR
TALES

TUDOR
TALES

TUDOR TALES

DAVE
TONGE

For Kim Voisey,
whose wonderful illustrations adorn my book

First published 2015

The History Press
The Mill, Brimscombe Port
Stroud, Gloucestershire, GL5 2QG
www.thehistorypress.co.uk

British Library Cataloguing in Publication Data.
A catalogue record for this book is available from the British Library.

ISBN 978 0 7509 6241 4

Typesetting and origination by The History Press
Printed and bound in Great Britain by TJ International Ltd. Padstow

CONTENTS

Introduction

ong before I ever became a storyteller I was a historian, burrowing into sixteenth-century court records, researching the relationships between men and women and looking at how they were dealt with in courts and how they interacted with each other. It was a revelation to me that we could know so much about our ancestors and I soon realised that Tudor people were not that different from us. They reacted to crises and related to each other much as we still do today. Their problems were different, but they were not.

When I became a storyteller, I found that there was a wealth of sixteenth-century 'chap books' and other cheap print available to me. From moral works to 'gest' books, as soon as I read the tales I realised that their themes and characters reflected those I had already found in my historical research. Yet again they show us that Tudor people were not that different from us!

More importantly, both the records and stories show us something of the reality of Tudor life, not the idealised version as seen in Acts of State and sermons of the time. Evidence often used to paint a picture of an oppressive society, where everyone knew their place. But that is an oversimplification of life long ago and although it was a patriarchal and hierarchical society, these were complicated times.

There were conflicting ideas and attitudes that can be seen in the records and stories I have included in this book. Long ago publishers were desperate to sell their wares to as big an audience as possible and included titles that would appeal to all, which means that for every story mocking a certain group there is also a reply, redeeming them!

The stories were adapted from older medieval sources such as the *Decameron* and *Heptameron* and were also taken directly from oral culture by printers who were always looking for new material to feed a growing audience for cheap print. Even though literacy levels were low, the stories could be read out in tavern yards and other public places, thus returning to the oral culture from whence they came.

Some of the medieval material appealed to people of higher status, focusing as it did on nobility, chivalry and adventure, but the old stories had little to offer the lower orders who preferred comic and often bawdy tales that still reflected something of their dreams, fears and desires. That said, cheap print was just that and some of the humour was coarse and unsubtle, while the ideas and attitudes within do not always sit well with modern tastes. They were, however, a welcome release from the tensions created by the conflict between idealised expectations and the reality of Tudor life, but more of that below.

As for this book, it is a work of two halves. First, the historical introductions, with a variety of records including many from the consistory courts, the church courts held in Norwich and also the city's mayor's court (all records are from the city sessions unless otherwise cited). Tudor Norwich was second only to London in size and wealth and so the examples from there are representative of any major town or city of the time. In addition, the court regulated many aspects of daily life, from what a person wore to the price of grain, family life, sanitary practices, moral lapses and even entertainment; thus it gives us a wonderful insight into Tudor society. This is me writing with my academic head on, although when it comes to the records, some of the spelling and punctuation has been changed for the ease of the modern reader.

The second half consists of the stories themselves and it is here that I write as the storyteller. Many of the tales were printed as simple anecdotes and jests in the sixteenth century, for the ease of the printer as well as to make them accessible to a semi-literate audience. Once storytellers got their hands on them, though, it was a different matter. Then, as now, storytellers 'grew new corn from old fields', padding stories out with their own experiences and adapting them to suit their audience. That's exactly what I do as a teller of tales and what I have tried to do with the stories below. Because many of the tales were drawn from oral culture and told aloud in Tudor times, I have attempted to give a feel of the telling in my versions.

I have also amalgamated some of the smaller stories into larger ones and created new titles where necessary in this, my book of two halves. Two halves, yes, but they come together to show you something of the ideas, attitudes and beliefs of our Tudor ancestors.

Thanks to Helen James and Debbie Handford for amending my terrible grammar. Also to Colin Howey for the use of his Norwich records and to Stewart Alexander for introducing me to the wonder of storytelling!

Dave Tonge, 2015

THE STRUGGLE FOR THE BREECHES

OF THE MUTE WIFE

n 1571, the author of *A Homily Against Disobedience and Willful Rebellion* denounced all kinds of rebellion including in families and households, stating that 'the wife should be obedient unto her husband'.[1] A few years earlier in 1568 the courtier Edmund Tilney had written: 'It is the office of the husband to deal and bargain with men, of the wife to make and meddle with no man.'[2]

Both these examples present an idealised image of women long ago, but statements such as these did not reflect the reality for many Tudor women who clearly took no notice of such advice; women such as Mary Wyer, the wife of Edmund, who was ordered to be 'sent to Bridewell and from there to the duck stool and there to be ducked three several times for scolding with her neighbours and other outrageous behaviour'. Also Alice Cocker, who was to be 'set in the cuckingstool as a common scold and brawler and a women of disquiet among her neighbours for that she did beat Ellen Dingle and Joanne Tymouth'. Both women were of course punished, but not for their scolding ways, rather for the antisocial behaviour that accompanied it.

Tudor society was a patriarchal society, but that does not mean that women did not have a voice, a fact that some men used to their advantage. As, for example, when John Elwyn was sent to serve a warrant on Henry Symonds, who 'did stay back and animate his wife who tore the warrant up and with lewd and unseemly speeches said, a turd in thy teeth, I thought the Mayor had more wit'.

Symonds was all too willing to exploit a women's subordinate position within the household and clearly many Tudor women were happy to speak their minds, a reality that's also reflected in stories from the time. Stories like the one below, a comic tale that deals with the troubles between husband and wife, or what was often termed 'the struggle for the breeches' …

In the fair and fine city of Norwich where I come from there lived a rich merchant, a man who made his coin by buying and selling wool. A thriving trade in the time of King Henry and his children and the merchant was skilled at his profession. So crafty was he that he had many great chests of gold in his counting house, but this rich merchant of Norwich was no miser. He loved to spend the chinks and so he bought a fair and fine house in the shadow of Norwich Castle. In that house he had fair and fine tapestries upon the wall and many not so fair and fine servants to do his bidding. The rich merchant wore fair and fine clothes, certainly much finer than any of you reading this story today! And that rich merchant also had himself a fair and fine young wife called Elizabeth.

Ahhh, Elizabeth! She was beautiful. Some said she was the most beautiful woman in the whole of Norwich, while others said no, she was the most beautiful woman in the whole of Norfolk, 'and you can't get fairer or finer than that!' The merchant, however, knew better, for he felt certain that she was the most beautiful young woman in the whole of Merry Old England. Perhaps he was right, for her hair was the colour of the brightest summer sun on the brightest of summer days. Her skin was as soft as duck down and as smooth as marble. Her lips were redder than the reddest ruby ever plucked from the earth, or the reddest rose ever plucked from the bush, and she smelt just as sweet.

Alas though, there was a problem with Elizabeth and the problem was this … she was mute. Never had a word passed her lips, which bothered the merchant greatly and he longed to hear her speak. He felt certain that if his fair and fine young wife could speak, then surely her voice would also be fair and fine. He felt certain that if Elizabeth could talk, her voice would match the birds singing in the trees, or even the very angels singing to the glory of God in heaven above. And so it was that he was sad that she had never uttered a word.

He was not, however, sad all of the time, for the merchant was a haunter of alehouses and loved a strong pot of ale when the working day was done. Each and every night you would find him in the alehouse with his many friends, but on this evening he arrived at the alehouse early and there was no one else about except for the alehouse keeper and a stranger to the city. A very strange stranger indeed, for when he thought about it later, the merchant could remember no detail of the man, save only that he wore a dark cloak and a dark hood which covered his face. And so they sat, the rich merchant on one side of a table, the stranger on the other and now they caught each other's gaze. The stranger glimpsed the sadness just in the corner of the merchant's eye and he asked him what ailed him, what had brought the merchant so low? The merchant said, 'I have the most beautiful wife in the whole of Merry Old England. Her hair is the colour of the brightest summer sun on the brightest of summer days. Her skin is as soft as duck down and as smooth as marble. Her lips are redder than the reddest ruby ever plucked from the earth, or the reddest rose ever plucked from the bush, and she smells just as sweet. But,' said the merchant, 'she is mute, she cannot speak and I wish that she could talk, for I feel certain that if she could talk her voice would match the birds singing in the trees, or the very angels singing to the glory of God in heaven above. That,' said the merchant, 'is why I am sad.'

Well, the hooded stranger began to laugh. 'Is that your problem?' asked he. 'Why, that's no problem at all.' And now the stranger reached into his pouch and pulled out a small bone, which looked like a human bone, perhaps from a finger or even a toe, but the merchant thought it better not to ask. 'Take this bone home and bind it with a lock of your own hair,' said the stranger, 'then place it beneath your sleeping wife's tongue for one hour before midnight, till exactly one hour after midnight. No more, no less!'

The merchant was so desperate to hear his young wife speak that he followed the stranger's instructions to the letter. At one of the clock in the morning he plucked the bone from beneath his sleeping wife's tongue. He kissed her gently and tried to settle down to sleep. But this night sleep would not find him, for he was desperate to know if his wife had won her voice. He was desperate to know if that voice was finer than the birds singing in the trees, or the very angels singing to the glory of God in heaven above. And so it was he sat up in bed and kissed his wife a second time upon the cheek. 'Wake, Elizabeth,' he whispered.

'Rouse yourself, Elizabeth, and talk to me.' Well, slowly, oh so very slowly, the merchant's young wife began to awaken in a most fair and fine fashion. Her eyelids fluttered in a fair and fine fashion. She sat up in bed and she stretched and yawned in a very fair and fine fashion. Slowly, oh so very slowly, Elizabeth turned to her husband and she spoke. It was the first time that the beautiful young woman had ever, ever spoken.

'WHAT DO YOU THINK YOU ARE DOING WAKING ME UP AT THIS TIME?' she screeched. And now she chided and scolded her husband, calling him fool and dullard and other outrageous oaths too lewd, earthy and Tudor to mention here. Her fair and fine mouth had become a dunghill of filthiness! She harangued her husband for a full hour or more, until he could bear it no longer. He rose early and went to his place of business.

But the merchant did return home that night, for he felt certain that given time both Elizabeth and her new tongue would settle some. Alas, though, as the days turned into weeks and the weeks turned into months his fair and fine young wife developed an evil disposition. 'WHAT DO YOU THINK YOU ARE DOING STAYING OUT ALL NIGHT?' she screamed, 'YOU THINK MORE OF YOUR FRIENDS THAN YOU DO OF ME.' Then there was her tongue – he had never seen a tongue as busy as hers and the merchant took to likening Elizabeth's tongue to a sharp blade, for every time she scolded him it cut that man to the bone! Oh how he wished he could sheath that knife. Oh how he wished that he could shut up his scolding wife.

Now if she had been the wife of a poor man she would have been ducked in the River Wensum, three times at the least, but as the wife of a rich man she was not. And so it was in desperation the rich merchant went in search of the hooded stranger and when at last he found him drinking in a tippling house of low credit, he fell to his knees and begged the stranger, 'Please, please, PLEASE, take back my scolding wife's voice!' But the stranger shook his head and said he could not. He stood up and throwing off his hood he spoke once more. 'Know this, rich merchant of Norwich. I am not really a man, for I am a demon from hell. And like any demon from down below I can work many wondrous spells including giving the gift of speech. But know this, rich merchant,' said the demon, 'neither I, nor any demon from hell, why not even the very Devil himself, can shut a woman up once she has started!'

Of the Contrary Wife

The Tudor family was supposed to function as a miniature state with the husband at its head, but a husband's power over his wife was not without limits. He could chastise her but excessive violence, as with other forms of abuse or neglect, was not sanctioned by the state and both violent and wayward husbands were punished. Robert Fellingham was set in the stocks for 'beating and misusing his wife' while the Tudor writer Edmund Tilney advised men like Fellingham against violence, saying that during an argument the husband 'must show his wisdom. Either turning it to sport, dissembling the cause or answering not at all.'[3]

There were limits to how and when a man could sanction his wife and for some men this was a cause of confusion and concern, not least because Tudor treatises on marriage could be ambiguous, often containing conflicting advice. The courtier Edmund Tilney, for example, stated that women should 'make and meddle with no man', but goes on to say that it was a woman's duty to 'govern her household'.[4] It was a role that could bring women into conflict with men and even the authorities, as in 1532 when twelve Norwich women were ordered to be whipped at the cart's tail for the 'selling of divers men's corn against their wills and the setting of prices thereof … contrary to such prices as the mayor has set'. This was seen as a serious crime, hence the harsh punishment, although in this case the whipping seems to have been commuted to a small fine instead. Was it recognition of the poor harvest and subsequent rise in the price of bread that year, but also perhaps of the ambiguous nature of female authority within Tudor society? Maybe it was, but it was not an authority that found much sympathy in stories of the time …

There was once a woman who chose to ignore the foolish prattlings of men who talked too much but never listened. As far as she was concerned it was her job to talk too much and never to listen to anything a man said to her, and she had grown skilled at her craft. The woman argued constantly with her husband and never before or since has there been such a contrary and quarrelsome a wife as she! From morning till night she opposed her husband in all things and she always had to have the last word. He had no choice in the matter, for more than once she had combed his hair with a three-legged stool! If her husband said it was light, she would say it was dark; if her husband said it was sweet, she would say it was sour; if her husband said it was thither, then she would say it was yon!

Well, one early morning, her husband rose from their bed and threw open the shutters to reveal a bright summer's day. The sky was blue, the sun shone and the bees buzzed busily about their business. The man breathed deep, stretched long and yawned loudly while scratching those places that all men go to first thing and then he spoke. 'It's a fair day for a walk, wife,' he said, 'and perhaps a picnic by the river?' But his wife sneered at her husband, calling him 'fool' and 'dullard', and she replied, 'The day is clearly foul, for there is rain in those clouds, far better to stay in our bed.' 'But wife,' said her husband, 'the day is fair.' His wife replied, 'The day is foul.' And so it was they fell to arguing … 'Fair!' 'Foul!' 'Fair!' 'Foul!' 'Fair!' 'Foul!' 'Fair!' Until at last her husband gave way to his wife and, as always happened, he let her have the very last word. 'The day is foul!' said she, triumphantly.

Nevertheless there was work to be done and now her husband suggested that they walk by the river, so that they might see how their crops were faring in the nearby field. 'If you come along,' said the husband to his wife, 'then it would be the chance you were looking for to wear the new blue dress I bought you at the last spring fair.' But his wife sneered at her husband, calling him 'blockhead and dunce', and she said, 'The dress you bought me last spring is green, not blue.' 'But wife,' said her husband, 'the dress is not green. It is as blue as the sky on this fair, I mean foul, day!' His wife replied that the dress was green. And so it was they fell to arguing once more … 'Blue!' 'Green!' 'Blue!' 'Green!' 'Blue!' 'Green!' 'Blue!' Until at last her husband gave way to his wife and as always happened, he let her have the very last word. 'The dress is green!' said she, triumphantly.

The argument being settled they went out for a walk, the wife wearing the blue, I mean green, or was it blue, dress. As they walked by the river they talked of many things and argued about even more until they came to the large fields where their neighbours were already hard at work harvesting their rye. And the husband, seeing that the grain had ripened, suggested that they too set to work cutting their crops. 'Wait here but a while, wife,' said her husband, 'while I run home and fetch us two well-sharpened sickles to cut our rye.' But his wife sneered at her husband, calling him 'clot-brain' and 'oaf', and she said, 'You can't cut the crops with a sickle, husband, for everyone knows that scissors are best!' 'But wife,' said her husband, 'you cannot use scissors to harvest your crops, for it would take weeks, if not months. The wind, rain and frosts would come and the rye would be ruined!' His wife replied defiantly, 'You definitely use scissors, not sickles, to cut the crops.' And so it was they fell to arguing again that day ... 'Sickle!' 'Scissors!' 'Sickle!' 'Scissors!' 'Sickle!' 'Scissors!' 'Sickle!'

But this time the dispute continued, for this time the husband could not give way to his wife. If he let her have the last word then he would have to cut the crops with scissors and that would take weeks, if not months. The wind, rain and frosts would come and the rye would be ruined! The husband turned his back upon his wife, ignoring her as he walked home along the river to fetch two sickles. But his wife followed close behind her husband unwilling to let him win the day. She skipped about him and whispered loudly in his ear, 'Scissors, scissors, SCISSORS!' until at last her husband could bear it no longer. He turned and pushed his wife into the river where she thrashed and splashed, for having been told by her husband that she should learn to swim, she had decided against it. She gurgled and gasped, but still she called out, 'Scissors, scissors, scissoooors,' as she sank slowly beneath the water. The woman sank and her husband smiled as he thought to himself, 'At last I shall have the last word,' and he called out, 'SICKLE!'

His triumph was short lived, however, for out of the water rose his wife's clenched fist. Before his eyes the fist unfurled to reveal two fingers. Two fingers that cut the air as they sank slowly back into the murky depths. And so it was, even in death the defiant women had the last word!

But that is not quite the last word from me, for the story did not end there. You should know that the arguing woman was even more contentious in death and as I heard tell, the wilful woman's body floated upstream against the current. Even the river could not get the better of the contrary wife!

OF THE GENTLEWOMAN
WHO HAD THE LAST WORD

omen spoke their mind long ago and regularly slandered men as well as other women. We know this because they often appear in slander cases before the consistory courts – which, due to the nature of the slanders, were often referred to as the 'bawdy courts' – long ago. Thus, Margaret Cock appeared for having slandered Lionel Wade, saying that he was an, 'old whoremasterly knave and japed Ann Kettle'. Ann Elcocks accused Wesson's wife of 'being caught upon the knee of a beer brewer with her clothes up'. Elcocks also said that Wesson was 'a wittol who received a barrel of beer for the use of his wife'.

Such extreme examples of slander were not just the preserve of the church courts; secular tribunals, such as the Norwich mayor's court, also dealt with cases, especially when members of the city elite were slandered: Margaret Caly was sent to the Bridewell because 'on Witson Tuesday last she did revile and miscall Christopher Giles and often times clapped her hand upon her backside and bade him kiss her there'.

The women above were punished for their insults, and while it might be argued that this is further evidence of patriarchal oppression, it is equally true that no matter how harsh the penalties, it did not serve to deter them. They continued speaking their minds, slinging insults in the marketplace, in the alehouse and even in stories like this one. However, unlike the gentleman in this tale, most men knew better than to argue with women, preferring instead to heed the words of Will Shakespeare in *The Comedy of Errors*, where he reminds us all that 'there's many a man has more hair than wit'.[5] …

There was once a young gentleman who fancied his wit was equal to that of Friar Bacon – a man whose renown was once so great that there are many tales told about him, one of which resides in the pages of this book. He was a much wiser man than the young gentle fellow who in truth was a coxcomb, not so much a man, but a youth who was conceited in character and vain besides!

Such were his failings that he failed to see them himself and he pranced about town like a peacock among his peahens, displaying his vanity for all to see and seeking to impress any young woman he met, although in time he met his match. For one day while drinking in a low tippling house that was frequented by many a gallant such as he, the gentleman fell to talking with a merry maid who saw beyond his fine feathers and preening ways. She looked upon his boyish beard, for although it was fairly full upon his top lip, it was but thin and wispy upon his chin. 'Why sir,' said she to the foppish fellow, 'you have a beard above, but none beneath.'

The gentleman liked not her words and sought to return them twofold. 'Why Mistress,' he replied, 'you have a beard beneath, but none above.' And he laughed at the quality of his jest.

But his wit was no match for that of the merry maid who made answer to his joke. 'Well, sir,' said she, 'if that is so, then we should set one beard against the other!' Such was her answer that I doubt that even the great Elizabethan playwright or even Friar Bacon could have replied, let alone a conceited coxcomb. The young gentleman was so shamefaced, his feathers so ruffled, that he said not one more word, but went instead to seek another peahen less merry and learned than she.

OF THE KNIGHT AND THE WIDOW

For the final story in this chapter I offer you a tale adapted in Tudor times from one of Aesop's fables. The story is of a widow, for many a young husband long ago died from war, dearth and disease, meaning that many women remarried. Although for some, like the Norwich merchant and mayor Thomas Sotherton, this was a cause for concern. When he died he left about eight thousand pounds, much of it to his wife as long as she was mindful 'of the mutual long love continued between us', and that she continue to 'have an especial care for the good of our children … hoping that no second love shall cause her to remove the most earnest promised love vowed and protested, as well as to me in private, as in the presence of some of our friends'.[6] In other words he didn't want his money being diverted away from his own family!

It is likely that Sotherton's wife didn't remarry and some women seem to have been happy to remain widows and run their late husband's businesses, either alone or with the help of family. That said, many did remarry to protect themselves in later life for it was not easy to be a woman alone in Tudor times. Perhaps that's why Abry Woolbred was whipped at the post 'for clothing herself in man's apparel and offering to go forth with the soldiers'. Her husband, Robert Woolbred, a weaver, had been caught drinking late at night, pressed into the army and sent to fight the Spanish. Was it simply a case that Abry could not manage the household and business without him or could it be an example of true love, that she just couldn't imagine life without her Robert?

Whatever the case you only have to read Shakespeare to know that it was not uncommon for women to disguise themselves as men. And in the ballad *Long Meg of Westminster* (1583) the heroine is presented as a strong woman who went to war disguised as a soldier and was eventually rewarded with a pension for life. But this ballad also reflects the ambiguity and unstable nature of women's position in Tudor society, for Meg eventually marries, promising her husband that she will never return his blows. She goes from being a strong independent woman to a submissive idealised image of womanhood.[7] The same ambiguity is reflected in this story, about a strong woman who desires another husband …

Once long ago there lived an alewife, an old woman who divided her time between selling ale and searching for her next husband. She collected husbands as other women collect pins, pots and potions from passing pedlars. The alewife had had more husbands than there were days in the week, but fewer than there were fingers and thumbs on both her hands, although whether it were eight or nine, not even she could remember! All of them had felt the sharp end of her tongue and all of them had felt the cold bony fingers of Death gripping hard upon their shoulders. In time he had come to claim them all and in truth most were happy to go. Her last husband had died just this very week and she was already searching for his replacement, a new man to take his place.

Well, it was on the very day that the alewife's last husband had died that a notorious rogue was hanged. He had been a thief and murderer of many years' standing, a man so skilled at his loathsome trade that his body was to be left hanging to rot, to serve as a warning to all other vicious vagrants who passed by. It was left to hang upon the gallows as a message to all who sought to steal and kill, but such was the notoriety of the hanged man that the lord of this place ordered a young knight to guard the corpse. He was to stand watch at the crossroads night and day to protect the body from any who sought to attack it or to steal it away, for who knows what grim purpose.

The young knight was new to his lord's service. He wanted to please the great man and so followed his orders faithfully. For three days and two nights the young knight never left his post, eating where he stood, napping only briefly against the gallows and using a nearby bush whenever nature called. By the third night, however, the young man grew weary of his post; he was tired and lonely, with only the crows for company. But the crows said little, for they were too busy pecking at the dead man's eyes and hair. They had little to say to the young knight and so when darkness fell he sought out the company of a gentler sort at an alehouse nearby. It was the alehouse of the recently widowed alewife, a woman who was also seeking gentler company this night!

The old woman was pleased to welcome such a handsome young man of prospects to her house and even more pleased to pour him many a pot of ale. More pots than there were days in the week, but fewer than there were fingers and thumbs upon both his hands, although whether it were eight or nine, not even the young knight could remember, for now he was drunk and he fell asleep upon a bench. He did not wake until the moon had done its work and the sun was thinking about taking over and it was only as a newly lit fire warmed his face that a chill passed over the knight and in a panic he returned quickly to the gallows.

His worst fears were realised, for even before he got to the crossroads he could see the hanged corpse had been stolen. Where once the body of a villain had hung, now only chains remained. He ran back to the old woman's house, for he knew only a few people in the town and trusted even fewer. The alewife had treated him kindly and he had heard tell that old women such as she were well known for their great wit and wisdom. He fell to his knees before her. 'Good wife,' he pleaded, 'if you do not help me this morning, then I must leave, lest my lord hang me for a knave in the dead rogue's place.'

The alewife was quick to act, for she had taken a fancy to the young knight. She thought him a lusty fellow and was not about to give him up so easily. She did indeed have enough wit and wisdom for the both of them and with spade and lantern she led the knight to the graveyard where her husband had three days' since been buried. 'Fear not, gentle knight,' said she, 'for if you do all that I ask of you this early morning, then you shall be safely delivered.' The alewife held the lantern high as the young man dug into her husband's fresh grave, for as the old woman said, 'we shall hang his body upon the gallows in the murderer's place!'

And so it was they dug up her dead husband's mouldering corpse and hung it about with chains. The old woman was well pleased with their handiwork, but the young knight was not. Something was wrong, something was not right, for now he remembered that the wretch who had hanged upon the gallows had had but one leg, for the other had been lost long ago when he had fallen beneath a cart. The old woman laughed. 'Tis no problem,' she said as she fetched a saw, her third husband's it was, and now she sawed off her last husband's leg!

The old woman was well pleased with their handiwork, but the young knight was not. Something was wrong, something was not right, for now he remembered that the wretch who had hanged upon the gallows had had but one arm, for the other had been lost in a fight. It had been cut off with a sword during

a brawl when he had been caught cheating at cards and dice.
The old women laughed. 'Tis no problem,' she said as she
fetched an axe, her fifth husband's it was, and now she hacked
off her last husband's arm!

The old woman was well pleased with their handiwork, but
the young knight was not. Something was wrong, something
was not right, for now he remembered that the wretch who had
hanged upon the gallows had had but one eye, for the other had
been taken by one of the crows that had stood watch with the
knight these three days past. The old women laughed. 'Tis no
problem,' she said as she fetched a dagger, her second husband's
it was, and now she plucked out her last husband's eye!

The old woman was well pleased with their handiwork, but
the young knight was not. Something was wrong, something
was not right, for now he remembered that the wretch who had
hanged upon the gallows had had a great scar upon his cheek,
for he had been branded by a court long ago. A mark had been
burnt upon his cheek to show all that he was both a liar and a
thief. The old women laughed. 'Tis no problem,' she said as she
fetched a red-hot poker, her seventh husband's it was, and now
she seared her last husband's flesh!

And so it went on, the old women knocking out her dead
husband's teeth, cutting off two of his fingers and mutilating
his body until it resembled the corpse of the murdering rogue
that had once hanged upon the gallows. The old woman was
well pleased with their handiwork and so at last was the young
knight. The alewife's dead husband was a goodly match for the
stolen body and the young knight fell to his knees and thanked
the old woman for her kindness, promising to reward her gen-
erously for her help this day. The old women smiled, for she
knew well what she wanted in return this day. 'I wish to be wed,
once more to marry,' she said, 'I wish for you to become my
husband and I to become your wife.'

Well, the young knight leapt to his feet and began running.
Leaping over bush and stream in great strides he called back to

the old woman, 'Wed you, goodwife? I will never wed you, for I have seen well enough how you treated your last husband. I'm off!' The young knight found an old horse and he galloped off, never to be seen in that locality again, while the alewife's last husband was left to rot. And as for the old alewife? Well, I've heard tell she brewed many more barrels of ale and collected many more foolish husbands before her day was done.

CHAPTER II

THE WORLD TURNED UPSIDE DOWN 1

'THE WIT AND WISDOM OF WOMEN'

OF THE GOODWIFE OF ORLÉANS

'The world turned upside down' refers to a growing fear in the late sixteenth and early seventeenth centuries that the established hierarchy was being eroded, especially when it came to the relationship between man and woman, husband and wife. There was a particular concern over female sexuality, made worse by the fact that for the first time in English history young women were spilling into towns and cities across the country; young women who were away from the traditional controls of father, husband or master and often described as 'living and working at their own hands'.

The authorities worried that these young were easy prey for any who wished to exploit them. Men and women like Wenfring's wife, who was set in the stocks for 'enticing young women to lewdness and suffering ill rule in her house'. She was a brothelkeeper, a bawd, and it was women like her who were accused of corrupting young women such as Elizabeth Moore who confessed before the Norwich mayor's court that she had been 'begotten of a child by William Dyer, a tailor in the house of Henry Brown, alehouse keeper who had the use of her body six weeks before Michaelmas last past and divers times after. She then keeping there and working at her own hands.'

Many were also concerned that the young women could themselves corrupt unwary men. Women like Mary Edwards, who was recorded in the court records as a 'single woman', who was to be 'whipped at the post for ill rule'. As any Tudor doctor would have told you, women were thought to be cold and phlegmatic and their humours thought to control the human body at the time were said to be wet and fluid, which made them unstable, fickle, naturally lustful, covetous and full of guile. Now we might not believe that today, but in Tudor times they did and it was a belief that was reflected in many of the stories as well …

Long ago and in the far-off city of Orléans there lived a good-wife who was handsome and lovely to behold. So pretty was she that I cannot do her beauty justice, but I will try. She was a peach and a poppet; her skin, it was as white as morning milk and as bright as a newly minted coin; and while most women walk to where they wish to go, she would skip and frolic like a newborn calf. She was a dolly and a daisy. She was as tall as a mast and as straight as a crossbow bolt. She was as slim and as a supple as a weasel! Need I say more? Probably not and so I will say only this …

The goodwife of Orléans had a 'come hither' eye and many men came hither. Not a problem, you might think, but you'd be wrong, for the young woman was married to an old man of business. A man of business and a man of great wealth, for he knew all the tips and tricks of his trade and he held all that was his firmly in his grasp. Like all old men with a young wife he had a jealous eye and he kept a close watch upon his young bride.

And with good cause, some might say, for there came to Orléans a young student of good bearing. He was of noble stock and fine humour and soon he found favour with all he met in the city, but not the old man of business. The young student spent more and more time at the old fellow's house and, being a good-natured lad, he quickly found favour with the old man's young wife. The goodwife of Orléans enjoyed the student's company and soon they fell in love.

Her husband, though, was no fool. He kept a sharp eye upon his wife, a keener eye still upon the lusty youth. He paid his servants to spy on them and before long heard tell that his young wife and the student had made arrangements, no less – that when the old man of business was next away the two lovers planned to meet; that when he was next away taking care of his trade, his young wife would send word to the student to meet her at the locked garden gate. There he should wait for her until it was dark and then they would be together at last!

It is a strange thing perhaps that a man can be happy and sad at the same time, for the old man of business was hurt by his servants' reports, yet joyful that he would catch his cheating wife in the act. And so it was he went straightaway to the young woman's chamber and told her that he must go away on business that very day. 'Wife,' said he, 'I must go far, far away, for many, many days, so be sure to look after my house, my dear and be sure to behave as a good wife should.' Having baited his trap the old man ordered his horse to be saddled, his bags to be packed, and he left.

Well, his young wife, having no knowledge of her husband's knowledge, sent word to the student to meet after dark at the locked garden gate. Her husband, having full knowledge of her plan, left his horse and baggage at a nearby inn, disguised himself with cloak and hood and he went early to the locked garden gate, where he waited and he waited. His wife in their house also waited until the servants had lit candles in her husband's hall and then she could wait no longer. She ran out of the house and down the garden path. Unlocking the gate she threw herself into her lover's arms. She drew him close and held him tight, but he shied away. And now as they walked up the garden path it was difficult to tell who was leading whom up the garden path! For the lover did not speak and would not look at the goodwife and she began to suspect a trap. The young woman dropped her handkerchief and stooped but a little to pick it up and as she did she glimpsed her husband's face. She saw that he had deceived her as she had deceived him.

It is a strange thing perhaps that a woman can be dismayed and downcast at the same time, for the goodwife of Orléans did not want to be caught, yet neither did she wish to lose the student's embrace this night. And so she grasped her husband firmly by his arm and led him inside. She took him upstairs to the highest chamber in the house, a dark damp room where she begged him to stay. 'Wait here but a while,' she said, 'and when my husband's servants have eaten and gone to their beds, then we shall be together!' The goodwife left, locking the door behind her, while her husband clapped his hands together and laughed loudly, pleased that he would soon reveal himself to his wife and punish her for her cuckolding ways.

But as the ancient proverb states, 'what the donkey driver wants is one thing, what the donkey actually does is quite another,' for having locked her husband in the chamber above, the young woman ran back down the garden path. She leapt through the garden gate and into the arms of her true love. They hugged, they kissed, they embraced and then she led the student into the house where the second comer fared much better than the first, for they went straightaway to her chamber where they hugged, kissed and embraced many more times!

Well, after many more hugs and any amount of kisses the goodwife left the student to rest a while and gather his strength, while she went to take care of the servants. She fed them upon her husband's best cuts of meat and let them sup his finest wines and when all were more than a little merry she called them together and in a most serious way told them of the lusty student. 'You all know well of the student who has oft times come to my husband's house,' said she; 'well, this very night of the very day that my good husband went away on business, the student has come again. He forced his way through that garden gate and he would have forced himself on me had I not tricked him, for now I have lured him to the highest chamber in the house where I have locked him in. And so,' she continued, 'this very night his day of reckoning has come. Go now all of you and beat him soundly. Whether he be standing up, sitting down, or lying on the bed, give him such a thrashing as he'll never darken my husband's door again!'

The servants needed no further telling for all were her husband's men. One seized a large stick, another a great club, one a sturdy staff and the other a stout cudgel and all four ran upstairs to the highest chamber where they burst through the door and went about their business beating the student, or rather their own master in disguise! So foul was the violence that night I cannot do it justice, but I will try. The servants pulled the bed sheets over the old man's head so that he could neither move nor cry out and now they beat him both above and below the waist and if any one of you had been there that night and had been able to keep tally of the blows that were struck, then I would consider you to be a better reckoner of numbers than I. None of the rough men were grudging in their blows and if the husband had paid a cleaner of clothes one hundred pounds, they could not have dusted his coat more thoroughly than his servants did that night!

Well, having beaten their master black and blue, the servants dragged his sheet-wrapped broken body down the stairs and cast it upon the dung heap outside, while their mistress returned to her own chamber and the student's embrace. They hugged, they kissed and oh so much more, until the moon was spent and so were they. Only now did the student return to his own lodgings for well-earned rest and as the sun showed its face that day the old man of business did too. He crawled off the dung heap and into the house and, feeling foolish that his plan had gone awry, he told servants that he had been attacked by vagrants upon the road.

His men took up their master and bathed his wounds, while telling the old man of how loyal his young wife had been. How she had protected her honour and dealt so harshly with the student and how proud he should be to have such a loving young wife. The old man of business was pleased to have such a good wife and ashamed to have doubted her. He swore an oath to his servants that he would never ever mistrust her again, while his wife also swore an oath that day – that she would never ever tire of the lusty student's embrace!

OF HE WHO PAINTED A LAMB

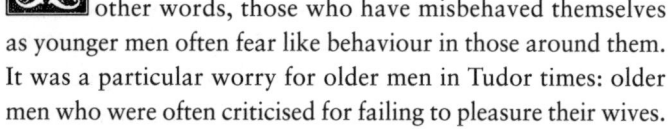

n *Henry VI, Part III*, William Shakespeare reminds us all that 'suspicion always haunts the guilty mind'.[8] In other words, those who have misbehaved themselves as younger men often fear like behaviour in those around them. It was a particular worry for older men in Tudor times: older men who were often criticised for failing to pleasure their wives.

The early seventeenth-century physician Thomas Johnson advised husbands that when they came to their wives' bedchambers, they 'must entertain her with all kind of dalliance, wanton behaviour and allurement to venery'.[9] Other doctors agreed that female sexual pleasure was a prerequisite of a happy relationship and the conception of children. It was often said that a woman who was not satisfied by her husband, or a maiden not yet in a sexual relationship, might suffer from the 'green sickness', a disease of the uterus that led to hysteria

Any man not able to satisfy his wife risked mockery and one of the worst insults a man could receive was to be called 'cuckold', a man whose wife had cheated on him, or 'wittol', a man who had knowingly been made a cuckold. So damaging was the insult that many men went to the consistory courts, the bawdy courts, to challenge such an allegation. Men like Richard Lucas who sued Alice and Cecily Walker for calling him a cuckold and for saying that 'he should go home and dry his pissed sheets'. Elizabeth Haver's husband sued Richard Dring for calling his wife a whore, 'whose husband is faint to keep house at home'.

The implication of these insults was clear to all long ago: a man who could not satisfy his wife lost control of his whole household. Thus, a man's inability to do his husbandly duty called into question his ability to run his business or even an important Tudor city like Norwich. That's what Robert Costen thought and why he was whipped in the Norwich Bridewell because at the Magdalene fair he 'did go up and down the fair, with a pair of ram's horns about his neck gathering a great company of lewd people to follow with clubs and staves and bagpipes, terming himself Mr Mayor and going from booth to booth and getting drink and shaking his horns, saying that they were his ruff.'

Ram's horns were the traditional emblem of the cuckold and often left nailed to an accused man's door, as part of communal mockery and punishment of cuckoldry, which helps explain why in stories at least, men went to extraordinary lengths to try and stop it …

There was once a clever painter from Breton who was a master of his craft and a man of older years whose daubs were famed for the look of the real world that he captured on his canvases. His portraits too bore a wondrous resemblance to all those who sat before his easel and those he painted were portrayed full of life, their eyes bright, their complexions lusty. Such was his skill that the painter was in great demand, whether it be painting a likeness of some ambitious alderman, or perhaps a hunting scene on a rich merchant's parlour wall. At other times he could be found illuminating a manuscript, a bible perhaps or other moral work for a mayor or a nobleman's wife. And sometimes he even contrived a miniature of some well-born lady to be kept close to a lovelorn lad's lonely heart.

Such was the master painter's skill that he was often called away to work his artistry in other towns and even far-off countries. He had as a younger man enjoyed the travel, sampling the delights to be found in far-flung places and enjoying himself all the more because he was working in towns where most did not know his name, nor could they tell his family and friends of his misdeeds, being so far, far away from home. But he was no longer a young man, travel no longer found favour with him, not least because he was at an age when over-exertion caused him to ache from the insides out. That was reason enough, you might think, to keep to hearth and home, but he had another cause more pressing still to travel no further than his studio set high in an attic room of his house, for the painter had recently taken a young wife who was comely to behold.

Like many of the young women you will hear tell of in this my book, she was beautiful. Suffice to say that she was prettier still than the pear tree in full blossom and the soft, sweet flesh of that particular fruit was no more sweet and soft than the flesh that covered her slim and wanton frame. Well, the painter had an artist's eye, he could appreciate beauty, but as a man who studied the detail in all things, he also had an eye for ugliness and all manner of evil behaviour. He saw it everywhere and having practised it himself long ago, he knew it well enough. How then could he continue at his trade, journeying wherever his skill with a brush was needed? How could he leave his wife alone to be admired by those who were not guided by their appreciation for beauty, but only by their base desires? He feared he could not, lest he find a way to protect the work of art that was his wife.

The answer was for his young wife to become his canvas, that she should herself take the place of the wood panels on which he so often practised his art. And so it was he lay his wife upon the bed and there did use all the cunning of his craft to paint a lamb upon the lower part of the young woman's belly. It was a rendering so finely wrought that none could lie with his wife lest both the image and his wife be defiled. It was an image so lifelike that if it was spoilt, then none could repair the damage nor replicate the lamb that he had crafted just below his wife's navel.

Satisfied that by painting alone he had protected his wife from the attentions of lewd and unseemly men, the master painter packed his brushes and boards and left upon his business. He left his wife to take charge of his household, his servants to care for his wife and a young journeyman painter new to his service to see to any small painting jobs that needed completing while he was away at his trade. But the young journeyman painter was not that willing to see to the commissions yet completed by his master and was far more interested in seeing to his master's young wife instead!

At first the painter's wife would not consent to his pleas, not least because she feared that her husband's artwork would suffer from the young man's attentions even if she did not. But she was as young as the journeyman and she too had needs and desires that her husband had trouble fulfilling when he was there and now he was not, well what could she do? For as everyone knew long ago, such unsatisfied young women's wombs were want to wander. It is hardly surprising, then, that eventually she relented to the young man's demands. At last he obtained her favour, at least six times before the Whitsun last past and diverse times thereafter!

With such attention to detail the painting of the lamb suffered greatly and soon the master painter would be returning home after two full years away. Their lusts sated, both the journeyman and his master's wife's thoughts turned to preserving their livings. And so it was that the journeyman painted a ram complete with long curling horns where once the lamb had lain upon the young woman's belly. And just in time, for the master painter came again to his house and went straightaway to see his young wife.

He used her roughly and demanded to see the lamb he had painted below her navel. 'Show me the painting,' said he, 'and then we shall have some fun.' Obediently his wife undressed and her husband looked at her belly. Seeing there a great horned ram he grew angry. 'What's this?' he cried, 'I painted a lamb, but now I find a ram!' His wife, having guile and cunning enough to put the trickster Howleglas to shame, replied, 'Why, husband, did you not know that a lamb so cunningly painted would grow into a ram in two years? If you had been a loyal husband and come home sooner, then you would have found a lamb still!'

And there the tale of he who painted a lamb ends. We must assume that the great skill the master painter displayed with his brushes was not matched by his wit and the workings of his head. For once again, a man's art was no equal for a woman's artful nature.

OF THE HUNCHBACKS
THREE AND ONE OTHER

On 10 September 1561 Agnes Leman appeared before the Norwich mayor's court accused of adultery with John Gorney and for her crime it was ordered that 'at one of the clock in the afternoon she shall be taken out of the prison and led about the market and so by my Lords house and over Coslany bridge and to St Georges and over Fyebridge with a basin tinked before her and so set upon the cucking stool and ducked in the water.' Hers was a shaming punishment that began in the marketplace, because it was here, of course, that the elite could guarantee the largest audience for the humiliation that was to follow.

Other punishments also took place there, including the stocks, pillory and cage, although it was also the location for all sorts of entertainment. In Norwich the City Waits, the corporation's own musicians, were ordered to play every Sunday night from the roof of the Guildhall, 'to the great comfort of the crowds'. Anyone frequenting the market on market day could expect to see puppet shows and plays about Robin Hood and Dick Whittington, or perhaps even an itinerant gymnast or some other wandering performer. These included a fortune-telling horse, a man who could 'perform great feats with his mouth' and also Provoe's wife, a woman with no hands who was allowed 'to show diverse works with her feet'.

It could be argued that women like Provoe's wife should be seen as a positive example of disability long ago, but there was a freak-show mentality to much of what was displayed, with spectators enjoying the misfortunes of others; especially in cases like that of Humphrey Brawley who was allowed to display 'a child having two heads'. Alas, the case of Provoe's wife is not enough to paint the Tudor people as enlightened individuals and the one thing that can be said about performance, spectacle and stories long ago is that a person with a physical disability was seen as a fair target, especially if they were a weak husband as well. Perhaps it is as well to heed the words of William Shakespeare when he reminds us all that 'beauty is bought by judgment of the eye, not utter'd by base sale of chapmen's tongues.'[10]...

Long ago in far-off France there lived a man who nature had wrought poorly, for he had been born with many deformities. He was small in stature and his back was bent and hunched, while his shoulders were broad, making him appear as wide as he was tall. I will not call him ugly without, for such things are in the eye of the beholder, but I will say that the hunchback was ugly within. For he was a merchant by profession, a rich man of business who, like another you will meet between these pages, knew all the tips and tricks of his trade and kept all that was his firmly in his grasp. The hunchback listed all of his belongings in a great ledger, including his young wife, for like many old men with young wives he had a jealous eye and regarded his bride as HIS property. As far as the hunchback was concerned his wife was akin to a painting displayed upon the wall of his cabinet, hanging there for his enjoyment only and not for the pleasure of others.

The young woman was beautiful and many had adored her. Her skin was as white as morning milk and had once been as bright as a newly minted coin, but no longer, for her husband had shut her away for his own solitary amusement. He treated his wife harshly and the young woman once so full of life was now emptied of all hope. She was kept under lock and key in a chamber set high in the hunchback's large house, much like a bird, trapped within a gilded cage and her feathers were already beginning to fade.

It had been a year since the hunchback and his bride had wed, but it seemed much longer to the young woman who spent her days staring out from her high window, watching the seasons pass and counting the dreary days. She had married the hunchback in late December and now it was December again. It was the eve of Christmas Eve and she could see many making merry in the streets beneath her prison, but their happiness never quite reached the bride at the window. She looked down upon the world beneath, but none below ever looked up to see the young woman weeping bitter tears down upon their heads. It seemed to the young woman above that everyone below was just far too busy having fun and thinking only of themselves.

Well, being Christmas there was much fun to be had and this very day a fair came to the town where the hunchback and his captive bride lived. There was a great procession of bright and colourful characters, beating drums, ringing bells, juggling knives and breathing fire! Their rough music reached up to the young woman's chamber and looking out she saw three tumblers tumbling, leaping over each other and her heart leapt too, for the three dancing acrobats were hunchbacks! They were much like her husband in looks, but oh so very different in their natures, for their hearts were full of joy and she could see that they brought great joy to others. One of the small hunchbacked players beat upon a timbrel, a small drum, while another played a merry tune upon a small bone pipe, while the third having no skill with music, did a little jig, a dance in the latest fashion.

So taken was the young woman with the hunchbacks below that she beat upon her chamber door, calling her husband and begging him that the three tumbling players might come up and entertain her for a short while. 'For just one hour, husband,' she pleaded, 'as a Christmas present for me!' Well, her husband's hard heart was softened a touch, as, looking out of the window, even he could not fail to be moved by the joyous rabble below. And besides the three hunchbacks did not threaten him – they were clearly ragged poor men, with humped backs like his and had little to offer his wife beyond their foolish feats. His heart hardened once more as he thought, 'They are ugly hunchbacks just like me and so my wife will be no more attracted to them than a cat would fall in love with a rat!' And so it was, seeing no harm in the hunchbacked players, the hunchbacked husband let them inside and paid each a few coins to perform for his wife.

The three tumblers leapt this way and that and the young woman was not disappointed as one of the small men beat upon a timbrel, while another played a merry tune upon a small bone pipe and the third having no skill with music, did a little jig in the latest fashion. The three hunchbacks' hearts were full of joy and they brought joy to others including the merchant's young wife. Such joy that time passed too quickly and the old hunchback returned to send the tumblers on their way. The three players left and so too the husband, for he had business in need of completion before Christmas Eve.

The young woman was alone again, but she could no longer bear it, for she could hear the three hunchbacked players singing and laughing below. She leant out of the window and begged them to come back and perform for her some more. She offered them her silver wedding ring, all she had, if they would but climb the trellis that passed close by her window. And climb the trellis they did. Soon they were performing for the merchant's wife again. Once more the three tumblers leapt this way and that. Once more one of the small men beat upon a timbrel, while another played a merry tune upon a small bone pipe and the third having no skill with music, he did a little jig in the latest fashion.

The young woman's pleasure was great, but alas short lived, for she heard her husband's key in the lock below and his footsteps upon the stairs. Business had been brisk that day and now the hunchback returned home. In a panic his wife hid the three tumblers in a great chest beside the fire, burying them deep in the blankets lest her husband should find them. The merchant, having no knowledge of the three players in the chest, decided to enjoy his wife this night and so there in the chest the three ragged hunchbacks remained lest they wake the fierce old man from his sleep.

Well, the following morning the old hunchback left early about his business to seal one more deal before Christmas Day. No sooner had he gone than his wife went to the chest to release the tumblers three, but the three ragged hunchbacks were dead, suffocated among the blankets. The young woman had hoped that they might perform for her once more before they went, but they would not play for her or anyone else again! Guilt hurt her heart, but also fear, for her husband would soon be home and she had three bodies to be rid of. The tumblers' corpses must go, but the young wife could not do it and she had but a silver wedding ring to pay another to do the deed for her.

Leaning out of the window she saw a stout porter about his business, a man who carried goods from here to somewhere else and seeing he had no load this morning the young woman called down to the man and offered him the ring if he would but rid her of a body that just happened to be in her house. While he climbed the trellis, she lifted one of the small hunch-backs from the chest and placed him upon the floor. She chose wisely, because the porter had many mouths to feed and was not that choosy about what he fetched and carried. He quickly stuffed the corpse into a sack, climbed back down the trellis, and because all were making merry in the town he was not seen as he went about his grim business. He hurled the first hunchback's body into the river, not even waiting to see if it sunk before he rushed back to the young woman's house to claim the silver ring.

Meanwhile the merchant's wife lifted the second tumbler's body from the chest and when the porter returned she would not give him the ring telling him that he had not yet done that which was asked of him, 'Look,' she said, 'no sooner had you gone than the hunchback returned! So this time do the job properly or you shall not be paid.' Well, the porter could not understand what was going on, but thought perhaps a pot too many of Christmas cheer had dimmed his wits. And so it was, he quickly stuffed the corpse into a sack, climbed back down the trellis and went about his grim business. He hurled the second hunchback's body into the river, not even waiting to see if it had sunk before he rushed back to the young woman's house to claim the silver ring.

Meanwhile the young woman lifted the third tumbler's body from the chest and when the porter returned she would not give him the ring telling him that he had not yet done that which was asked of him, 'Look,' she said, 'no sooner had you gone than the hunchback returned again! So this time do the job properly or you shall not be paid.' Well, the porter could not under-stand what was going on, but thought perhaps a pot too many of Christmas cheer had dimmed his wits and even dulled his senses. And so it was he quickly stuffed the corpse into a sack, climbed back down the trellis and went about his grim business.

He hurled the third hunchback's body into the river, although this time he waited to be sure that it sank. He cursed the hunchback loudly, for he had better things to do this day than hump a humpback thither and yon. He watched as the body sunk into the murky depths, warning the corpse that had better not surface again, 'This time you can go to the Devil,' he said, 'and if you come back from the dead again, then you'll be sorry.' The porter shook his fist for good measure and rushed back to the young woman's house to claim the silver ring.

But as he neared the young woman's house the porter saw her hunchbacked husband returning home. The porter looked and looked twice more, for there was the hunchback, returned from his watery grave and now the labouring man crossed himself. The porter had never been a religious man, but he feared that it was not the ale after all causing the dead to rise this day! So true to his word the porter did the job himself this time. He took a cudgel from his belt and struck the old man of business about his head, scattering his brains and waiting a while to see if the dead man had plans to rise again! On this occasion he did not and for a fourth time the porter stuffed the corpse into the sack and went about his grim business. He hurled the merchant's body into the river and waited the rest of the day to make sure he rose no more.

Satisfied at last that his cudgel had done what nature could not, the porter returned to the young woman's house, where she gladly handed over her silver wedding ring. After all, she had no further need of it and all that had been her husband's was now hers. The young widow was saddened at the loss of the tumblers three, but happy to be rid of a man who had been far uglier on the inside than he had ever been without. She was happier still knowing that her cage doors had been thrown open and now at last she was free.

OF THE PARTRIDGES AND THE PRIEST

 omen went out into the marketplace where they would have to deal with wayward men, but sometimes trouble came into their own homes, even occasionally in the guise of a priest.

Suffice it to say, men of God were capable of all sorts of 'evil' and 'ill behaviour'. And even though the Tudor Reformation may have rid England of greedy friars and lusty monks, it did little to save us from knavish priests who hid their sins while preaching of goodness to others. That's why the Parson Robert Serton was brought before the church courts in Norwich, where he stood accused by Hammond's wife that he 'would resort to her house almost daily with many sundry excuses such as the buying of eggs and that he would say unto her servants that he came to fetch a kiss from them and did by these lewd practices endeavor to abuse them'.

Serton clearly lacked the ability to govern himself as a godly man should, something that is reflected in the story below. In a time when the Church was in crisis, many would have enjoyed the priest's fall from grace as much as the wit and wisdom of the wife ...

There was once a man who was a poor but very pious farmer, who had little to hold on to in this world except the promise of a better life in the next. Such was his desire to reach the hereafter that he honoured the Church daily and so it was, one morning after prayers, he went hunting. In truth, spoils were thin on the poor man's land, but this day he caught two partridges who had made the unfortunate decision to nest in his hedge. This was clearly a sign from God, for the most he had ever caught before was a brace of coneys or a hare if he was lucky. A goodly feast like this was rare and so naturally he wished to share it with the one who was closest to his heart – the parish priest! For the pious poor farmer thought that surely the priest had played some part in his good fortune. He felt certain that all his prayers must have helped.

The farmer took the partridges home and told his wife to cook them while he went to fetch his honoured guest. 'See to our supper, wife,' said the farmer, 'and do not let a morsel of it pass your lips!' His wife knew better than to argue with her husband and so she set them on a spit to roast by the fire. Well, the farmer's wife fancied herself a good cook and so thought it wise to see how the partridges tasted. She took a pinch of skin and it tasted good. Being the wife of a poor man she knew better than to dream of great wealth, but when all was said and done she did not shy away from fulfilling her own desires! The skin tasted fine and the juices bubbling beneath were sweet on her tongue and so it was she attacked the first partridge as if she had not eaten in a month of Sundays or more. Soon she was licking her fingers and wondering what she would say to her husband. How best to explain the missing bird? She thought perhaps she might blame it on the cat; her husband would believe that. The poor farmer's wife pondered upon her clever excuse, made all the more brilliant because she knew the cat to be an unreasoning selfish beast. A creature much like herself, for he too did not shy away from fulfilling his own desires. Indeed, so selfish was the cat that the poor farmer's wife felt sure that he would have eaten both birds. So certain was she that there was nothing else to be done. Grabbing the second partridge, she would have swallowed it whole had her not her tongue and teeth dictated that she chew a while first!

Well, having eaten both birds, the poor farmer's wife began to think that blaming the cat had not been a good idea. If she blamed the cat her husband would most likely kill the old tom and she did not fancy adding the catching of mice to her already busy days. There was to be no easy answer and the poor farmer's wife was still licking fat from her fingers and pondering her fate when her husband returned, rushing home ahead of the priest to make sure that all was right and proper for the arrival of his honoured guest. 'Are the partridges cooked?' asked the poor farmer as he busied himself tidying their small home. 'Oh, they are, husband,' replied his wife, 'and now they are resting a while in the meat keep while I make a sauce well suited to partridge.' The poor farmer's wife wanted to get rid of her husband and so she sent him into the garden, there to set the table. For as the wise woman said, 'it's a fine day to eat outside in the orchard and you wouldn't want a priest of such great learning to be confined by our four small walls, would you, husband.' Then she suggested that he take the carving knife and whetstone with him. For as the wise woman said, 'the partridge is a fine meat and you wouldn't want to serve a man as sharp as the parish priest with a dull blade!' The poor man heeded his wife's words and went into the garden where he began to sharpen the naked blade.

It was now that the priest arrived at the poor farmer's house and, seeing his wife alone, the priest thought that he might partake of a starter. He took hold of the woman and while the poor farmer whet his knife upon a stone without, the priest was trying to whet his appetite within! But the poor farmer's wife pushed the priest away, not alas out of any loyalty to her husband, but because all her pondering had at last borne fruit. The wise wife bid the priest leave now. 'Make haste,' said she, 'for my husband knows. He knows that you wish to fulfil your desires with me!' And now the poor farmer's wife showed him the empty spit in front of the fire. 'There never were any partridges,' said the wise woman and she pointed to her husband in the garden sharpening his knife. 'My husband made them up to lure you here and he plans to castrate you this day. He is going to cut off your cods so that you never feel the need to embrace another man's wife again!'

The priest looked out the window at the poor farmer sharpening his carving knife and he needed no further telling. Scooping up his vestments he ran from the house, while the farmer's wife went into the garden and told her husband that the priest had stolen the two partridges. 'The bird had flown,' said she, 'and he has taken two more birds with him!' The poor farmer was angry. All his life he had followed the teachings of the Church. He had been mindful of sin, while the priest it seemed had only been mindful of his belly. With carving knife in hand he gave chase and seeing the priest in the distance he called out, 'Stop priest stop, for by God I'll take them both,' meaning the missing partridges. The priest, however, hearing the poor man's words, thought that he meant two things far more valuable to a lusty rogue such as he and so he ran faster still. The terrified priest leapt over the graveyard wall and into the church, where he barred the door against all who tried to enter and as far as I know he never accepted another invitation to dine again!

Of the Lady Prioress
and the Three Lusty Knaves

Mischief begets Mischief

The stories thus far in this chapter have told of husbands desperate to stop their wives' adultery and protect themselves from accusations of cuckoldry. But the situation was more complex than that and men walked a tightrope when it came to their own behaviour. On the one hand they had to be able to pleasure their wives, but on the other, men of higher status were also preoccupied with mastering themselves.

In a hierarchical society obsessed with status, self-mastery was seen as a way of differing yourself from the poorer 'lower orders'. In other words, a man's ability or inability to govern his own behaviour was used long ago to promote political and social exclusivity. If a man did not succeed in demonstrating his reason, he could be accused of misgoverning himself; of being a 'rogue', a 'saucy knave' or even a 'whoremaster'; and just like accusations of cuckoldry, the slander might see him being mocked by his neighbours. In the ballad *The Witty Maid of the West*, for example, a miller tries to lure a young maid to his chamber, but is instead lured by her into a bed full of nettles and chopped horsehair! The ballad ends with the miller being 'jeered by all that him know'.[11]

So damaging could an accusation of sexual misbehaviour be that many a man protected himself against such slander at the consistory courts. Men like Edmund Prettye who sued John Reeve for accusing him of 'frequenting the company of William Tarrold's wife'. Reeve said that Prettye 'salted after her as a dog did salt after a bitch and did humber after her as an old horse did humber after a mare'. Martha Cambridge said that Benjamin Wright was 'a saucy knave and a cunning knave who did come drunk or drunker into her house with his bobble hanging from his breeches like a horse'.

There was a known link between sexual misbehaviour and drunkenness; yet another form of unreasoned behaviour to be avoided if possible. As the Tudor pamphleteer Philip Stubbs stated: 'a man once drunk with wine or strong drink rather resembles a brute beast than a Christian man. For do not his eyes begin to stare and to be red, fiery and foam at the mouth like a boar.'[12]

Such was the concern over self-mastery among the Tudor elites that in Norwich, for example, aldermen and other councillors were fined if they were caught at any plays that promoted 'the allurement to vice and sin'. Such was the fear of dishonour that the authorities could and did punish their own. The Norwich Alderman, Nicolas Davey is a good example: 'For the evil behaviour among the citizens, as for that he hath suffered the open shame of riding in a cart about the city for the abominable sin of whoredom from this day forward shall be accompted none of the livery, but to be discharged from the same company and his livery taken from him.'

Men at all levels of society, be they poor man or alderman like Davey, were mocked and punished for misgoverning their bodies, which made it yet another wonderful subject for a story …

Many of my tales are about lusty friars and greedy monks whose devotion to God was far outweighed by their devotion to their base desires. And so by way of a contrast I would like to tell you a story of a nun whose virtue was well known to one and all. She was celebrated for her purity, honesty, kindness and charitable works, all good virtues only matched by her good looks, for she was the fairest of women as well as prioress of her convent.

Her modesty was well known, but it did not stop some men testing her daily. There were three in particular who lusted after her and were sorely tempted by her smiling eyes. It was all the prioress could do to protect herself from shame and she laboured hard upon the task. First there was a young knight who had yet to master his body, then came a priest of the parish, who had yet to master his mind. Finally, a burgess of the bor-ough, a married merchant who had given up trying to govern himself long ago! Each wanted to use her naughtily and so sent her presents daily, from freshly slain bucks and cunningly wrought brooches to bottles of fine scent and good wine. The lady accepted none of them and shut her doors to all three. She was growing tired of the game and working so hard to protect her modesty brought her low. Then she had an idea.

She invited the young knight to dine with her and let him prattle on about unrequited love and his yearning, burning desires. He talked of slaying mighty giants and Christian ene-mies in her name and of how he would kill himself if she did not return his affections. In truth the goodly nun listened little, for she had other ideas on her mind. When at last he had finished droning on the nun took his hands in hers. 'My lord,' she said, 'fret no longer, for I will be yours this night as long as you do all that I say.' The young man swore he would, upon his oath as a knight, kissing his sword excitedly to make the point. To see him caress his weapon so was off-putting to the nun, but she had started this journey and there was no going back. 'Go then from this place,' said the good woman, 'and wait for me in the ruined chapel. Lie there as still as a dead man until dawn, wrapped in a winding sheet so that none can see you move.' The knight agreed, for such was the strength of his desire it overruled what little sense he owned. Off he went with a winding sheet to play dead in the ruined church.

No sooner had he gone than the lady prioress sent for the priest telling him that she needed to talk with him on a most private and sensitive matter. The priest came quickly to her, for naught would have kept him away. She feigned interest as he wittered on about the Lord's heavenly plan and the sanctity of a union between man and woman, ignoring the fact that she had already wed herself to God and he too had made a vow of chastity. When at last he finished his pompous preaching, she took his hands in hers. 'Sir,' she said, 'my cousin has died and lies in the ruined chapel near here, for he departed this world in debt and so his family are not able to bury him. I have sworn to assist my family and so, Sir, if you help me then I shall return the favour.' The priest swore he would lend a hand and kissed her ring excitedly to show that he was willing. To feel his cold wet lips against her flesh was off-putting to the nun, but she had travelled a way now and her destination grew close. 'Go then, my good cleric,' she said, 'lay my cousin in a grave and say the burial rites so that he may go to heaven.' The priest agreed, for while his wits slumbered still, his lusts were roused and off he went with mattock and shovel to bury the waiting corpse.

As soon as the priest had gone, the lady prioress sent for the burgess, telling him that his presence was eagerly awaited. She smiled sweetly, even remembering to flap her eyelids as the merchant prated on about consolidating their two families through marriage and of how such a merger would be good business, forgetting that he was already married to another! When at last he had finished babbling on about buying a new wife, she took his hands in hers. 'Master merchant,' she said, 'know that you are my only friend, for the priest has gone against my word and this very night plans to bury the body of a knight who owes me coin, so much gold that I had forbidden his burial. So if you love me as you say, you will prevent the rite and punish the priest for his disobedience.' The merchant swore to assist his true love, he spat upon his palm and shook the hand of the lady prioress to demonstrate his resolve and seal the deal. The touch of cold spittle against her warm skin was upsetting for the innocent nun, but her labours were near complete and she wished soon to rest, and so the prioress suggested that the burgess should disguise himself as the Devil, 'to leap thither and yon like a fiend from hell!' The burgess agreed, for he thought it a bargain, to sate his lusts without having to pay out any reason on his part! He dressed himself in horns, red rags and chains and set off to the old church to petrify the priest.

The burgess burst into the chapel as the priest's funeral dirge was done; red-faced and roaring and rattling his chains he leapt this way and that, shrieking loud enough to wake the dead, including the knight who was playing dead! If the young knight was terrified, the old priest was petrified and he jumped through a window of the old chapel sorely hurting himself upon the broken glass. The young knight had been distressed enough hearing the priest say a funeral rite, but now that the Devil had joined the fray, he could take no more. He burst forth from the winding sheet and followed the priest through the broken window screaming loudly as he went. The burgess, seeing the dead knight rise up, ran away too, wailing as he went.

The priest ran one way, the knight another, and so too the burgess. All three running blind and bleeding through thorn and thistle, sparing neither high hill, icy stream, nor dense dark woodland as each fled from the other two. All hid in dark places that night, in ditch and den, bower and barn, and the following day when the sun was up and the fear had left them just a little, one by one they returned to the fair lady prioress, each in turn telling her their tales of woe; of nearly being buried alive, of meeting the Devil himself and of how the dead did rise in the night. And so it was that the nun was able to remind all that mischief begets mischief, and the bloody marks upon their bodies were evidence enough of that. She warned them all that what they had endured was a portent, a curse even, for she 'had never yet taken a lover who had died a good death!' The lady prioress said as much to all three, although she also threatened the burgess that she would tell his wife of his adulterous adventures, the bloody marks upon his body being evidence enough of that. She was only silenced by his promise to pay twenty marks that day and to draw up papers leaving much of his property to her nunnery when he was dead and gone.

There was once a nun who was celebrated for her purity, honesty, kindness and charitable works, all good virtues only matched by her good looks, for she was the fairest of women as well as prioress of her convent. A lady, then, who was well suited to her esteemed position, for she cured three men of their love sickness and secured her nunnery for many years to come.

OF THE POOR GENTLEMAN
AND HIS HAWK

If the other tales in this chapter show us anything, it is that there was a real concern over sexual promiscuity in Tudor times. A fear that it led to diseases like syphilis, called the 'French pox' long ago, while many also worried that it diverted funds from the household, leaving wives and children in want and higher poor rates for the rest of a community. As when Thomas Alyard, a notorious drunkard, was sent to Bridewell for 'living dissolutely' and ordered that he 'stay in the Bridewell till he find sureties that he will pay his wife 4 pence weekly'.

There was an equal concern that sexual misbehaviour led to bastardy, meaning the birth of illegitimate children who were likely to become a burden to the poor rates. Bastardy legislation became increasingly harsh over the sixteenth and early seventeenth centuries, with expectant mothers being forced to name the fathers of their babies before midwives would help them with their 'great travail', while the reputed fathers, or 'bastard getters', could be held in prison till they found sureties to support their illegitimate offspring.

So great were these fears that church sermons abounded with images of male sexual depravity, with one such homily likening adultery and whoredom to 'a most filthy lake, foul puddle and stinking sink, whereunto all kinds of sins and evils flow', while reminding men that 'whosoever comitteth whoredom sinneth against his own body'.[13]

Tudor doctors also spoke out against male sexual immorality, with William Vaughn claiming that it 'harmeth a man more than if he should bleed forty times as much,' while Thomas Logan advised men to curb their lusts by sitting on a cold stone floor![14] Doctors saw such lusts as evidence not only of a physical disorder but also a mental one; lust led to unreasoned behaviour and made men little better than brute beasts, something that was also said of love: as Shakespeare tells us, 'love is your master, for he masters you; and he that is so yoked by a fool, methinks, should not be chronicled for wise.'[15]

It is, then, fitting that the last tale in this section is positively Shakespearian in its tragedy. Originally a medieval story, but reworked in the sixteenth century, it is the story of a poor gentleman whose falcon is the only evidence of the wealth and position he once enjoyed, for while a poor man might hunt with a sparrowhawk or goshawk, in a society obsessed with hierarchy, the poor gentleman's gyrfalcon was the preserve of the nobility, albeit a nobility lost to love …

Long ago in far-off Italy there lived a young man of noble birth, fine stock and good character. He was a gentleman with a gentle soul, who was well set up in life and had all that his heart desired, save only for a wife to share in his good fortune. That's not to say that he was not in love; he was, but that was where his fortune ended, for his love was a lady who was already wed. The object of his desire was married to a knight of the realm and they had one child, a boy of about seven or eight years of age.

Alas, the young gentleman's love was in love with another, but that did not stop him from trying to impress her. He spent most of his money hoping to amuse the lady, to try and catch her eye. Most of his inheritance was spent on fine, fancy armour that he wore at the tilt, the joust where young gentlewomen went to seek out a husband. He bought the finest tailored clothing his dwindling finances allowed. Fancy clothes they were and he wore them at court dances in the vain hope that the lady would notice him. He wore tight-fitting doublets of velvet slashed through so that all could admire the silk, satin, and sarcenet lining and he was noticed, but not by his lady. Never once did she look upon the young gentleman, never once did she return his love.

His only solace was his hunting hawk, a gyrfalcon, the finest, noblest and most expensive of all the birds of prey and one that only a man of his status could fly. When not wooing his love at court, the young gentleman would be out in the fields working his prize falcon, watching her as she swooped high one way and darted low the other. Smiling joyfully as the bird glided swiftly over the grassy meadows, cutting the air like the sharpest of blades. Sometimes no more than a distant speck, a strange shooting star in the firmament, until her wings tucked back and like an arrow spitting forth its poison, she dived, slamming into her prey with strong, sharp talons gripping it tight. The young gentleman's gyrfalcon never missed its prey, be it duck, pigeon, coney or what ever else she fixed her eye upon, just as her master had fixed his eye upon a married woman and now he could not let her go. Often he wished he could, especially when he was flying his gyrfalcon, for when working his fine bird of prey he admired her grace in the air and wished he could be as free as her as she rose up high into the heavens above.

He was not free though, for a madness came upon him whenever the lady was near. The lack of control that came over the young gentleman both frightened and elated him in equal measure. Certainly none who knew the young gentleman thought him wise any longer, for love had truly trampled upon his wits. Such was his lack of mastery over himself and his purse also, that his fortune was spent. The last of his sanity had left, taking his chinks with it! The poor gentleman had no choice but to leave the court and city and retire to a pauper's cottage in the countryside where none would see his shame. He took only his prized gyrfalcon with him, his only solace, his only friend in an increasingly cruel world.

Well, time passed and a terrible sickness fell upon the court and city, killing many including the lady's husband. Her son was also stricken and so it was the lady took flight. She left both court and the city far behind her and moved into a large house in the country overlooking meadow and field in the hope that the clean air would cure the ailing boy. But it didn't and slowly the affliction threatened to take the boy from his mother. The doctors could not tell what ailed him, for was it the illness that had claimed so many, or was it the loss his father that was sucking the life from the boy?

No one knew for certain, but it was noticed that the boy rallied when watching a poor man working his hawk in the fields below. His spirits lifted as he watched the gyrfalcon as she swooped high one way and darted low the other. What a poor man was doing with such an expensive bird, no one knew and none cared, for the lad seemed to forget all his troubles as he watched the bird glide swiftly over the grassy meadows, cutting the air like the sharpest of blades. The boy smiled joyously as the hawk became but a distant speck, a strange shooting star in

the firmament, until her wings tucked back and like an arrow
spitting forth its poison, she dived, slamming into her prey with
strong, sharp talons gripping it tight. This was a quick natural
death, unlike the disease-ridden slaughter the boy had seen all
about him in the city and while he watched the gyrfalcon work
it was as if his ailment left him and he was cured. But when
the poor man took the bird away to his cottage, the sickness
returned and the boy was forced to his bed once more.

It was strange that a poor man should have ownership of
such a noble birth and so the lady sent her servants to find out
more of this poor fellow who worked his hawk in the meadows
below. News soon reached her that he was the gentleman who
had run away from his troubles. Hearing his name the lady was
heartened, for she knew at last how she might save her dying
son. She had not forgotten how the young gentleman had often
made advances to her and how he had professed to love her so.
It was simple, then: she would ask the poor gentleman if she
might buy his gyrfalcon, for he clearly had need of the money
as she had need of the bird. But the lady had not forgotten
how she had spurned his advances, how she had often ignored
him and how he been driven to madness and fallen on hard
times because of his love for her. But the lady's concern for the
young gentleman's feeling was well matched by the love she
felt for her son and so she sent her servant to the gentleman's
poor house asking that she might dine with him, for she had a
favour to ask.

The young gentleman was overjoyed. It seemed that the lady
had come to her senses and would at last be his! But for all his
joy the poor gentleman was worried, for now his fortune was
spent and he had no money left to entertain a noble lady. He
could not provide a feast that was fitting of someone of her high
birth. He cursed his ill luck, but was not yet ready to lose his
love a second time. So he sent the servant back to his mistress
with a message that he, the poor gentleman, would receive her
at dusk.

The following evening, the lady arrived at the poor gentleman's home and appeared not to notice the few mean sticks of furniture and the lack of comfort within. They chatted about this and that while both shared a simple dinner and he did all he could to please her, listening intently as she told him of the death of her husband and the sickness that had brought her only son so low. And then the lady began to talk of the poor gentleman's hawk and how her son's spirits lifted as he watched the gyrfalcon swoop high one way and darted low the other, of how the boy seemed to forget all his troubles as the bird glided swiftly over the grassy meadows, cutting the air like the sharpest of blades. She told the poor gentleman how her son smiled joyously as the hawk become but a distant speck, a strange shooting star in the firmament, until her wings tucked back and like an arrow spitting forth its poison, she dived, slamming into her prey with strong, sharp talons gripping it tight.

The lady told the young gentleman how her son's life was as one with the bird and asked if she might buy it for her boy. 'If the falcon were his, then I feel certain my child would soon be well again,' said the lady with tears in her eyes, 'and if the falcon were his, then I shall forever be in your debt.' But the poor gentleman fell quiet, while the smile he had worn all evening wore thin. A single tear fell from his cheek as he fell to his knees. Finally he spoke. 'Know this, my lady,' he said, 'I would gladly give you anything I own to win your love, but I cannot give your son my gyrfalcon. For knowing that you were to dine with me this evening I have already given you that which I prized most in this world.' And he cast the falcon's hood and hawk bells upon the table by the emptied dinner plates. The gentleman turned his back upon his lady and walked away from that place, leaving it forever.

CHAPTER III

THE WORLD TURNED UPSIDE DOWN 2

'MASTERLESS YOUTH'

OF THE BROTHER WHO FOUND A CHEST

The Tudor period was a time of turmoil with religious, political and social upheaval on a scale hardly witnessed before. Death and disease were never far away and life was a struggle especially for the poorer sort. The ruling classes also felt an uncertainty about the future and many feared that the tumultuous times further eroded the traditional order, not just in terms of men and women, but also when it came to the young.

As vagrancy increased throughout the sixteenth century, so too did the perceived problem of 'idle young' and 'masterless youth', who were said to spend all their time in alehouses and getting up to all kinds of 'evil rule'. There is some truth in this, although it just demonstrates that Tudor teens were much like their twenty-first-century counterparts! Robert Balliston, for example, got up to some bonfire hi-jinks and admitted before the mayor's court that he and two other lads 'did yesterday take away a door of Arthur Cordy that was tied with string and the said John Brand did cut asunder and then carry the door to the bonfire where they burned the same'. On another occasion a master was summoned before the court because his apprentices 'did cast up rockets into the air whereby there was great fear that the houses would be fired'. Nothing changes!

Such was the concern that Bridewells were established to 'set loiterers and other idle persons to work ... and for ... the practicing of youth to be trained in work and the fear of God.'[16] As with the situation between men and women, the relationship between the old and young was more complex than the statutes and court cases would have us believe. Yes, it was a time when it was seen as beneficial to be harsh with the young, to keep them under control, but that does not mean that the young were not cared for. When Robert Brown, a twelve-year-old from Suffolk, was found lying in the street in Norwich, Robert Saborne 'being moved with pity took him to his house, gave him meat and drink and clothes and promised to take him as his apprentice weaver'. A few years later an apprentice, George Gooch, was released early from service, because he was 'enticed by his master to lewdness and also very much abused and evil handled by his said master'.

The conflicting attitudes towards the young is best summed up in the case of James Brown, a nine-year-old vagrant from

Cambridge, who was whipped out of Norwich with a pass to return home just as the law stipulated. But before he went, he was held at the Bridewell and the keeper there was ordered to supply the lad with new clothes and shoes for the journey. It's a conflict that also appears in Tudor stories like the one below, where differing opinions about youth are voiced; where the young are both vilified and celebrated. When we take into account that publishers of cheap print sought a willing audience among apprentices and servants, it's easy to see why tales like this one were so popular …

There was once a farmer who had lost his wife many years before, but still he had two full-grown sons. They were boys, young men really, who were both alike in looks, but oh so very different in their natures.

The eldest lad, John, was always up early and about his business. He was up with the lark and working in all weathers. John rose so early that he was up before the first cockcrow of the morning. In fact he rose extra early just to ensure that the cockerel had awoken, so that it could awaken everyone else! The lad was strong and quick and so all who knew him called the boy 'Lusty John'.

John's brother Jack was a completely different cut of meat altogether, for he spent most of his time lying in his bed. He was a weary lad and often his ancient father mocked the boy, calling him 'an unwiped, tardy gaited, bed-presser', harsh words long ago! The old man compared Jack unfavourably with his elder brother John and often went to the lad's chamber, shouting, 'Jack, you sluggard. You should be more like your brother John.' But Jack never listened. Instead, he would stretch and yawn, turn over in his bed, turn his head to the wall and go straight back to sleep. The lad was weak and slow and so all who knew him called the boy 'Lazy Jack'.

Well, it was winter and one morning early John went down to the bottom field and set to work with plough and oxen, turning the damp cold earth. And because he started early John finished early so that there was time enough to do other things. And so it was his father was pleased, yet vexed that his younger son had not helped. The old man went straightaway to Jack's chamber, shouting as he went, 'Jack, you sluggard. You should be more like your brother, for this morning he has ploughed the whole of the bottom field. You Jack should be more like John!' But Jack did not listen. Instead, he stretched and yawned, turned over in his bed, turned his head to the wall and went straight back to sleep.

Well, winter turned to spring and one morning early John went down to the bottom field and set to work seeding the land, broadcasting grain thither and yon over the recently harrowed earth. And because he started early John finished early so that there was time enough to do other things. And so it was his father was happy, yet irked that his younger son had not helped. The old man went straightaway to Jack's chamber, shouting as he went, 'Jack, you sluggard. You should be more like your brother, for this morning he has seeded the whole of the bottom field. You Jack should be more like John!' But Jack did not listen. Instead, he stretched and yawned, turned over in his bed, turned his head to the wall and went straight back to sleep.

Well, spring became summer, yet there was a waft of wood smoke in the air heralding autumn's return and one morning early John went down to the bottom field to harvest the crops. He worked hard, bending low, cutting close to the earth with a newly sharpened sickle. And because he started early John finished early so that there was time enough to do other things. And so it was his father was merry, yet galled that his younger son had not helped. The old man went straightaway to Jack's chamber, shouting as he went, 'Jack, you sluggard. You should be more like your bother, for this morning he has harvested the whole of the bottom field. You Jack should be more like John!'

But Jack did not listen. Instead, he stretched and yawned, turned over in his bed, turned his head to the wall and went straight back to sleep.

And so it was, life continued on this way for the old man and his two sons, John up with the lark, while Jack was down with his sheets. Summer soon passed, autumn was quickly spent and winter made a triumphant return. John continued rising early, for so lusty was the lad that he even left his bed when there was naught to do. He strode out over the cold, dark fields, leaping over frozen streams and climbing the bare branches of tall trees, just because they were there. And so it was one frosty morning John walked many miles, leapt many fences and raced many a surprised hare, but now his belly barked angrily telling him it was time to return home for his breakfast. But as John passed by the bottom field he saw a chest that had fallen on to the track on which he now walked. It was a chest full of gold, spilling its contents into the ditch that ran alongside the track. Once the chest of a rich merchant, containing a full year's profits from his trade, but it had fallen from his cart that very morning and now it was John's!

The lusty lad scooped up the gold and set the great chest on his shoulder, carrying it home for his father to see. And when the old man saw the gold he was joyous, yet incensed that his younger son had not helped John carry the heavy load home. He went straightaway to Jack's chamber, dragging the heavy chest behind him and shouting, 'Jack, you sluggard. You should be more like your brother, for this morning he has found a chest of gold. An unlucky merchant lost it this very day, but his loss is our gain and now we are rich. And that is why you, Jack, should be more like John!' As always Jack did not listen. Instead, he stretched and yawned, turned over in his bed, turned his head to the wall, but this day he did not go straight back to sleep. For the sun was shining and its light spilled through Jack's bed-chamber window and played upon the gold coin piled high in the chest, so that it was reflected on to the wall just above the lazy lad's head. The boy blinked as golden dancers spun and twirled about him. He rubbed his eyes and looked over at his father, to the treasure and back to his father again and then Jack spoke. You should note that this is the first time in a long time that Jack had spoken, for words take effort and thinking of the words to speak is even harder still. 'But father,' said the boy, 'if the merchant who once owned that gold had stayed in bed as I do now, then he wouldn't have lost his coin would he? If that rich merchant had been as lazy as I, then he would not now be poor!' And with that Jack stretched and yawned, he turned over in his bed, turned his head to the wall and went straight back to sleep.

Of the Father Who Bequeathed a Gallows

n the first story in this chapter we saw that there were ambivalent attitudes towards the young, but concerns over their well-being only went so far. When a boy called Edward Bushel was 'sent to Bridewell to be set to work', it was also ordered that he 'would be carefully looked into (for) he is a very bad one'. Robert Thenylthorpe was also sent to the Bridewell for running away from his master and for that he 'behaved himself very lewdly', while Henry, the servant of Master Garter, was sent to prison there to remain with a block upon his leg, 'for disobedience and drawing a dagger on his master'. Another apprentice, William Cheney, was set in the stocks 'for that he did break his master's head', although his master was also imprisoned for not reporting the offence, and allowing the boy to subvert the natural order!

Both master and servant were meant to know their place, although that's not to say that a servant's obedience to his master could not be punished if it conflicted with wider authority: as in the case of Pullen's boy who was whipped with a rod in the assembly chamber of Norwich Guildhall for 'going about to pick a lock of the prison door where prisoner Pullen lye'.

Punishments could be harsh for apprentices who fell out with their masters: William Bannock ran away from his master three times, and on the third occasion was sent back to him with 'pot-hooks' about his neck, while an act of 1547 made it legal for a master to mutilate and even enslave a runaway servant once caught. It was however repealed in 1550 for being too extreme.

Other methods were used to control the young and in Norwich, for example, they suppressed the annual 'Throwing at Cocks heretofore used by boys in this City.' It seems to have been a gambling game where lads threw stones at a loose chicken and the first one to hit the unfortunate bird won the pot. The fear was that such games quickly got out of hand and led to fights and even riots. After all, the authorities were well aware that young men were often at the forefront of disturbances in the city, as when Richard Todd and a number of other unnamed youths were described as 'idle disposed persons', and ordered to be 'whipped in the guildhall for committing various disorders and that they did pluck up certain pails and rails'.

It seems that they were leading a protest against the enclosure of common land and although it was considered a serious offence it is worth noting that Richard and company, like Pullen's boy above, were to be whipped inside. They were not to be shamed outside as older men or women would have been, a recognition of their young age and further evidence of the differing attitudes towards the young that are played out in the story below ...

There was once a father who lay dying, but no death is easy and nor was his. For the gentleman had bequests to make to his three sons, two of whom were gentle in nature, but as for the third, well, you will have to wait and see.

The dying man summoned his eldest son to him and the lad fell to his knees besides the old man's deathbed, sorely grieving over his father's faltering health. His father reached over to the boy, stroking his hands and spoke. 'You have always been a good lad,' said he, 'biddable in all things and happy to lend a hand and so I bequeath to you all my lands, from estates big to my city tenements small – all are yours, my son.' But his eldest son fell to sobbing, saying, 'Nay father, for I pray you shall live long and have use of the lands yourself.'

Next, the dying man sent for his second son, who fell upon his father, embracing the old man gently, lamenting his unhappy state. His father reached over to the lad, stroking his cheek and spoke. 'You have always been a good boy,' said he, 'slow to judge others, yet quick to help all those in need and so I bequeath to you all my movable goods, from the bedstead I lie dying in, to my best gown and trestle table – all are yours, my son.' But the second son he too fell to weeping, saying, 'Nay father, for I entreat the very angels in heaven that you will live long and have use of your goods yourself.'

Well, finally the third boy came before his ailing father so that he too might receive the old man's blessing, taking hold of his hand and sighing, mourning the gulf between father and son. The dying man drew away his hand from the lad and spoke. 'You have always been a stubborn boy,' said he, 'a lad of evil condition and lewd behaviour and so I bequeath to you neither lands nor goods, but only the gallows standing at the crossroads on the very edge of my land. It and it alone is yours, my son.' The boy had been cursed by his father, but now his son cursed the old man back. 'Nay father,' said the boy, 'for I implore the Devil himself that you live a long while yet and have use of the gallows yourself!'

And so it was that the old man died and the youngest son was forced to make his own way in the world, which was not an uncommon occurrence long ago. I only hope that he prospered, had children of his own and that he learned from his father's mistakes.

OF THE FRIAR, THE BOY AND HIS STEPMOTHER

hen the enemies Richard Carlton and Henry Bloye met upon the road one day they fell to arguing, as enemies so often do. Voices were raised; maybe even fists flew, especially after Carlton said of Bloye, 'if I had a turd in my hand I would give him leave to chew it'.

Tudor people often used insults that referred to bodily functions, for they were no more wedded to their waste than we are today. Don't be taken in with images in books of people casting the contents of their 'piss-pots' out into the streets in Tudor times. In truth, anyone caught doing such a thing could be subject to harsh penalties. In Norwich, the city bellmen called out daily, reminding all to 'cast out water on to the streets' and sweep in front of their houses daily. Those caught fouling the city were dealt with quickly, as when James Lowe was set in stocks because he did 'bury a necessary in the castle dikes.'

If you haven't worked it out already, our baser functions are something dealt with in the story below, along with the conflict between old and young, which in the story is made worse by the fact the young hero becomes a minstrel of sorts. They were also a group treated harshly in Tudor times and were often accused of spreading the plague and malicious gossip! Men like Thomas Spratt, a minstrel threatened with the pillory if he did not return to his wife in Colchester and further ordered that he should leave 'the roguish life of minstrels'.

This is an interesting case, but a mere curiosity in this story, for the real concern below is with the boy and his stepmother. Stepmothers were often portrayed in fairy tales as the 'baddie', a role that stemmed from concern over remarriage and the diversion of funds from the husband's first family. In this story, the boy's new mother is presented as the archetypal 'wicked stepmother' who threatens the lad in a time when violence against the young was, perhaps surprisingly to some, not tolerated. That's why Priscilla Johnson was ordered to be 'put in the stocks for beating and misusing a little girl in her service, and banned from keeping children at home'. Also, Agnes Rogers and Cicely Rogers, who, 'for most cruelly beating Robert Thorp, a little boy, for knitting, were both whipped at the post and Cicely is sent to the Bridewell'. Unfortunately violence towards the young was not uncommon, but it was dealt with quickly as in the case of Christian Aston who was accused of attacking her servants. It was said that they were 'grievously beaten and salted after they were beaten'. One was sent home to her father and another two placed in the Bridewell until new masters could be found for them, while Aston was whipped and also banned from keeping servants.

There are many examples of masters and mistresses being punished for assaulting their servants, but few when it comes to parents and their children. Perhaps because the family was said to be like a miniature state with the father as its ruler, it was more difficult for the authorities to intervene. That said, stories like this one do seem to show that violence towards the young, be it servant, son or daughter, was not much tolerated …

There was once a husband who had had two wives, but only one son. Jack was the boy's name, and such a good-natured lad was he that his father loved him dearly, although his stepmother did not! She thought Jack was as motley-minded as her new husband and was jealous of the bond between father and son. The woman was shrill tongued and oft times berated Jack's father for spoiling the lad, warning him that no good would come of it. She meant it, for Jack's stepmother kept a sharp eye upon the both of them and frequently used her even sharper tongue upon her husband, blunting it often upon the simple man's dull wits.

Jack's new mother was so wilful that she wore the breeches in their house. She made her new husband her 'cot queen' – a man who took over the household tasks. He had little choice, for his wife wanted everything her own way. So he took to sending his son out early to care for the cows in the meadow if only for his own comfort, to say nothing of Jack's. The work was hard, but the lad was happy in the fields, although he thought that his stepmother would be far better suited to bird scaring than he. He often imagined her scaring winter back into autumn and autumn back into summer and beyond. 'With a face like hers,' thought Jack, 'she could turn back time!' Often he wished he could go back so that he could tell his father not to marry her in the first place.

But this is a folktale, not a fairy tale, so wishes when they are granted are often strange and wondrous in form and just a bit naughty besides! For this day Jack had been toiling in his father's fields till noon, the sun was hot, the lad was tired and so he sat a while, eating his lunch. As always, it was a mean affair that his stepmother had packed for him. Just a few scraps and other leftovers from the table, but it was food just the same and Jack ate briskly, while whistling as was his way.

Well, it was now that a beggar passed by, a poor man with a back bent low by time and a beard so long that it dusted the track as he walked along. He was so old that even young Jack could see that he had less of the road in front of him than he did behind. The old beggar's clothes were threadbare and his frame was thin, but his smile was full and his eyes were so bright that his life-lined face shone like the high summer sun and warmed Jack's heart. It was obvious to the boy that the beggar had not eaten for a while and so he offered him a bite. The old man gladly accepted, quickly swallowing the last of Jack's leftovers. Then he thanked the lad, offering him three gifts in exchange for his kindness. 'After all,' said the beggar, 'one good turn deserves another, so know this, Jack, whatever you want in this world, it shall be yours!'

Jack scratched his head, for in truth he wanted very little, although, 'Perhaps,' said he, 'a bow would be good, to shoot the odd bird for my father's supper.' The old man nodded and from beneath his cloak he pulled out a bow and six arrows.

A fine bow it was too, for as the old beggar told the boy, 'this bow and these arrows will never miss their mark. Use them well, Jack, but not before you ask another boon of me.'

Jack scratched his head, for in truth he wanted very little, especially now he had a magic bow, although, 'Perhaps,' said he, 'some pipes to play might be nice, to banish the loneliness of sitting all day in the fields.' The old man nodded and from beneath his cloak he pulled out some pipes. They were subtly crafted, for as the old beggar said, 'these pipes will always keep time and all those who hear them will lose mastery over their bodies and dance as they have never danced before. Use them well, Jack, but not before you ask one more favour of me.'

This time Jack did not scratch his head, for he knew full well enough what he wanted most of all and told the poor beggar of his shrewish stepmother. 'Her sharp tongue,' said Jack, 'is only matched by her sharp eye and she keeps that firmly fixed on me!' The old man laughed and pulled out his left hand from beneath his cloak, clapping it hard against his right and winking knowingly at the boy. 'Say no more, Jack,' said he, 'for when next your mother uses her edged eye or tongue upon you, she will let rip a fart so ripe you will think that it has fallen from a medlar tree whose foul rotten fruit are fit only for making jelly!'

Jack was a happy lad and thanked the poor man in the style of the day, saying, 'God bless and keep you, sir,' while bowing for good measure. The old man returned the bow and went whistling on his way. And when the old man had disappeared over the hill Jack began to play upon the pipes, while the cows began dancing merrily as cows have never done before. He danced the cows all the way back to the barn and went straightaway to tell his father of the beggar who had naught to his name, but three strange and wondrous favours. His father was like many of you, for he loved a good story and he passed Jack a capon for a tale well told.

But Jack's stepmother was watching and it grieved her sorely to see the boy growing fat upon her efforts. She stared hard at the lad, but no sooner had she fixed him with her eye, than she let rip a fart like no other. It was a thunderclap of a fart that was so loud both father and son fell to laughing. The more they laughed the harder Jack's stepmother stared and the harder she stared the louder her farts! Until at last her husband had had enough. 'Be off with you, wife,' said he, 'and be sure to take your stinking arse with you!'

The women scolded both father and son, but it was her arse that replied and in truth made more sense! She stormed out of the house, while the shutters flapped in the grievous wind she left behind her. The windy wife went straightaway to her friend, a friar who had much in common with another friar who lives within the pages of this book, a man whose religion was food and the eating thereof. While the friar ministered to her soul, Jack's stepmother ministered to his belly, for the friar was a rump-fed artless fellow, a gorbellied lubberly man. He was lout-ish in manners and clumsy in manner, well suited for friendship with the woman. She told him of her belligerent belly and that Jack had Beelzebub himself inside of him, saying to the friar, 'It is your duty as a man of God to beat the Devil from the boy.'

The friar nodded, for if his head was wavering over the issue of possession, his belly was in full agreement with the woman. The following day he followed Jack to the fields where he aimed to purify the boy's spirit with a few well-aimed blows. But the friar was as wide in girth as Jack was tall and try as he might, he could not catch the boy. He chased Jack over field and fen and about many a tree and tussock until eventually even Jack got bored with the game. The boy stopped running and pointed to a pheasant perched in a far away tree whose boughs ranged out over some fierce looking brambles, 'If you stop chasing me,' said Jack, 'then I'll shoot the bird for your supper.' He fitted arrow to bow, he leant, he aimed, he shot and as the old beggar predicted Jack's aim was true and the bird fell dead into the brambles below, 'Be quick, Friar,' said Jack, 'lest a fox take your supper.'

The lubberly lout needed no further telling. He raced over to the tree and reached carefully into the brambles, while Jack picked up his pipes and began to play a merry tune. The friar twitched and the friar jerked while his legs took on a life of their own. What little mastery the friar had of his body was now lost to him as he began to dance wildly into the thorns, the brambles wrapping themselves about the corpulent cleric while he skipped about like a giddy girl! Suffice to say that the friar leapt high into the vicious shrub and writhed low out the other side. Then Jack danced the exhausted man all the way home, making him pirouette down the main street of the town, bare arsed and bloodied.

Such was the sight that many a young person laughed, but older folk did not see the joke. Even Jack's father thought that the lad had gone too far this time, for like many long ago, he held the religious in high esteem. To make your stepmother fart was one thing, but to make a fat friar frolic, well, that was quite another! He yelled at the boy, threatening him with his fists, but Jack did not care. Instead he picked up his pipes and began playing louder still, accompanied by the cries of all those who were forced to join the merry dance and his stepmother playing upon her billowing behind. A merry din mirroring their disordered behaviour. Rough music if ever I heard it!

The louder Jack played, the more people joined the romp, for none could resist Jack's tune, not even the leaden-footed, tardy-gaited types like another more lazy Jack, whose story is also told in this chapter of my book. And so it was, that our pipe-playing Jack danced one and all through the town until he got to the Guildhall where he made the mayor and his aldermen leap about the council chamber until the floors creaked and the ceilings cracked. He made them caper one way and cavort the other until they swore that no punishment would befall the boy if he but ceased playing so lustily upon his pipes. Jack agreed, but only if they also vowed to cure his stepmother of her evil behaviour, which they did with the aid of a ducking stool and a river running fast, cold and clear.

A cruel punishment I know and for my part I would have preferred that it was Jack himself who cured his stepmother of her jealous eye. Instead of ducking her in the river, I like to think that he made her dance a while longer, the lad playing merrily upon the pipes, while she jigged thither and yon, staring hard at her stepson and letting rip many a ripe fart. Although whether she kept in time with Jack's pipe I cannot say!

OF THE BEST FORGOTTEN

n 1565 it was ordered that Thomas Ebottes should no longer 'receive or maintain any man's servants, apprentices or others neither by day nor by night to the intent to keep any evil rule and use or exercise any unlawful games prohibited by the laws or statutes of the realm within his house'. William Rochester was imprisoned for 'keeping a dancing school and harbouring and receiving men's servants into his house to lodge'. The authorities were desperate to control the young, wanting them to work rather than play, and often they banned plays and other performances that would divert the young from their toil.

The following story, though, is about a young woman who had little interest in plays, performances or dancing with poor serving men, for she was a dreamer rather than a doer and she had her eye on greater riches than any poor boy could provide. But the story still functions like many of the harsh laws above, for it is a moral tale that promotes hard work, while warning against unchecked female desires ...

There was once a young woman whose life, like so many others long ago, was hard. Her family was poor and she had to toil long hours working on her father's few meagre strips of land. Her father could not help as he had been wounded in a war long ago. He spent most days now lamenting a young king called Henry who fought the French just so he could know glory and power like the kings of old. Her grandfather could not help, for war, famine and disease had taken their toll upon him. He was blind and couldn't see, he was lame and couldn't walk and spent his days lying by the smoky, smouldering fire with only the hard earth floor to serve as a bed. The girl's mother could not help, for she had any amount of work to do already – spin, spin, spinning wool into thread; thread that she would weave into fine cloth; fine cloth that would be cut and stitched into even finer clothes that she would never, ever be able to afford. And so it was the girl worked upon her father's strips of land alone, from dawn when the sun comes up, to dusk when the moon takes over.

Well, now it was dusk and the moon cast eerie shadows across the fields. It was time for her to return home. But as the girl made ready to leave her work a mist formed about her feet; a mist that began to boil and bubble, bubble and boil, to rise up and take shape. Before her eyes the mist became a man, but not just any man, for it took the form of a monk. He was once a man of prayer, once a man of care, once a man of joy and song, but no longer, for he was dead! He was a ghostly monk, a monk who was a ghost hovering above the surface of the land. In one hand he held out a great iron key, while with the other he beckoned the girl forward. He spoke. 'Come, child, follow me, for I shall lead you to great treasure!' So it was the girl followed the monk into darkness, she followed him into the night, lured on by the promise of coin and lots of it!

They walked and they walked and they walked, over the fields and through the woods, well beyond the places that the girl knew. They walked and walked and as they walked, thorn and thistle tore at the bottom of her skirts and the flesh of her bare legs, but neither thorn nor thistle touched the monk's ghostly gown as he glided across the surface of the land. They walked and they walked and they walked, until at last they came to a wide but shallow stream. The girl hitched up her skirts to tread carefully across lest she fall in the stream and soak herself, but the ghostly monk, the monk who was a ghost, simply glided across the surface of the water. They walked and they walked and they walked, until at last they came to the ruins of a priory. It had once been a place where monks had lived. Once a place of prayer, once a place of care, once a place of joy and song, but no longer, for it had been stripped of its wealth by a young king called Henry so he could know glory and power like the kings of old.

The ghostly monk, the monk who was a ghost, led the girl across the ruined priory ground until they came to some low trees. Beyond the low trees was a large stone wall. Set within that wall was a large wooden door and set within the door was a large iron lock. The ghostly monk, the monk who was a ghost, took the iron key from his belt, turned it in the lock and slowly, so very slowly, the door creaked open. And even though it was still dark outside the girl could make out something sparkling and shining brightly from within, for the chamber beyond was filled with treasure. There was gold, silver and jewels spilling from great chests and covering the floor. The girl walked into the chamber, closely followed by the monk. He set the iron key upon a chest and spoke these words, 'Take whatever you will, child, but remember this, you must take that which is best. Do not forget that which is best!'

Having no sack the girl began scooping handfuls of silver into her dress, for surely, she thought, 'there can be nothing better than silver!' As she began pulling the coins into the front of her dress she began to dream of how she would spend them upon her father. 'With these silver coins I shall buy my father meat,' she thought. 'No longer shall he live upon a pottage, a soup of peas and beans, and no longer shall he drink ale, for now he will drink wine – sack wine, flavoured with sugar and honey.' As she dreamt her dreams of sweet and sickly wine, she continued raking the coins into her dress, but now the ghostly monk, the monk who was a ghost, spoke again, 'Take whatever you will, child, but remember this, you must take that which is best. Do not forget that which is best!'

And so it was the girl began scooping handfuls of gold coins into her dress, for surely, she thought, 'there can be nothing better than gold!' As she began pulling the coins into the front of her dress she began to dream of how she would spend them upon her grandfather. 'With these gold coins I shall buy the old man a bed,' she thought. 'No longer shall he lie upon the cold, hard earth, for now he shall rest upon a soft feather mattress, a mattress resting upon a carved wooden bed.' And as she dreamt her dreams of soft feather mattresses and cunningly carved oak, she continued to rake the coins into her dress, but now the ghostly monk, the monk who was a ghost, spoke again. 'Take whatever you will, child, but remember this, you must take that which is best. Do not forget that which is best!'

The girl began scooping handfuls of jewels into her dress, for surely, she thought, 'there can be nothing better than diamonds, rubies and emeralds!' As she began pulling the jewels into the front of her dress, she began to dream of how she might spend them upon her mother. 'With these jewels I shall buy my mother a new dress,' she thought. 'I shall buy her one hundred new dresses, one thousand new dresses and each will be sewn with threads of silver and gold and decorated with fine lace and fur.' And as she dreamt her dreams of fine cloth, artfully stitched, she continued to rake the jewels into her dress, but now the ghostly monk, the monk who was a ghost, spoke again, 'Take whatever you will, child, but remember this, you must take that which is best. Do not forget that which is best!'

But the girl's dress was now full. She could take no more and so with a dress full of chinks and a head full of dreams she staggered slowly out of the chamber. But no sooner did she walk outside, no sooner did she walk out into the moonlight, than the treasure disappeared. The gold, silver and jewels, the diamonds, rubies and emeralds were gone, and so too the wooden door and the ghostly monk, for the girl had not taken the best. She had left the best behind. The girl did not know that which was best and now the question is this: Do any of you? One clue might be in the words uttered by the monk just before he disappeared: 'Do not be blinded by your greed!'

Still not got it? Then I suggest you return to the beginning of this story. To the woodcut that complements this tale, for there you will surely find the key to this riddle – something that would have allowed the poor girl to visit that treasure-laden chamber again and again and again!

CHAPTER IV

THE WORLD TURNED UPSIDE DOWN 3

'POOR MEN WILL SPEAK ONE DAY'

OF ADAM BELL, CLIM OF THE CLOUGH AND WILLIAM OF CLOUDESLEY

In Tudor England there were strict sumptuary laws relating to the clothes a person of a certain status could wear; it included their colour, style and the cloth from which they were made. The laws even regulated the food a person could eat and the hawk with which they could hunt and all to help maintain the strict hierarchy that was considered the lynchpin of Tudor society. Many fell foul of the legislation, including William Collard, a cobbler, who in 1551 was taken in the streets of Norwich for sporting a beard in a time when the laws dictated he should not. He was held by Alderman Davey who insisted that he should shave, but Collard replied that he would not, because, 'once he had been evil shaven and would not suffer it again'. But Davey was not satisfied with Collard's excuse and the two men fell to quarrelling. It was then that the cobbler was heard to say that Davey was 'picking on a poor man', and warned him that 'poor men (will) speak one day'.

Comments such as Collard's were a great cause of concern for city authorities, the wealthy merchants and other professionals who made up the ruling elite. Major rebellions like the Pilgrimage of Grace were not that uncommon in Tudor England and in Norwich, Alderman Davey and his peers would have well remembered Kett's Rebellion of 1549, where over 20,000 rebels set up camp just outside of Norwich and took control of the city for a while.

The rebels, many of them poor men, were protesting against enclosure, the loss of common land, but were eventually slaughtered by the Earl of Warwick and his mercenary army, while their leader Robert Kett was hanged from the walls of Norwich Castle. His body was left in chains over the winter and into the following summer, but even brutality such as this did not stop the poorer sort like Collard from challenging the authorities. In another case before the mayor's court, Robert Barwyke was imprisoned because he 'went to a certain alehouse where he had unseemly words both of nobleman and the magistrates of the City'.

There are many examples like those above and most caused by high prices and low wages, poor harvests and growing vagrancy in Elizabethan England that led to increases in poverty and terrible overcrowding in urban centres. The Norwich census of the poor of 1571, for example, found eleven families living in one house in a poorer parish of the city.[17]

With the tensions caused by poverty and overcrowding growing in Tudor England it is easy to see why the poor were so willing to give voice to their frustrations and why they enjoyed tales like the one below. The story of Adam Bell and his friends was very popular in Tudor times, focusing as it does upon popular insurrection against corrupt rule. Like the stories of Robin Hood, the tale of Adam and his associates represented and reflected popular discontent and showed that in stories at least, poor men could speak out and make their mark in the world ...

Many of the stories in my book tell of the south of our country long ago. Of places where the land was farmed or fenced off for the raising of sheep, southern regions where men and women wove cloth in small attic rooms and where there were great towns and cities in which rich merchants bought and sold and grew rich. But this story takes us north to wild places, where men raided cattle across the borders of Wales and Scotland, land yet to be dominated by great industrial cities. Instead it was still governed by great castles that had taken root over the generations and guarded the wild borderlands. For this is a time when the English were often at war with the Welsh and the Scots – and anyone else who crossed them, for that matter. And this was a time when many of the great men who ruled those northern castles and fledgling northern towns, be they noblemen, sheriffs or chief justices, were still at war with each other, all vying for yet more land and power far away from the royal court in London.

But this is not a story of great men. Instead it is a tale of three low-born lads like me! Their names were Adam Bell, Clim of the Clough and William of Cloudesley, who lived as brothers, good companions whose loyalty to each other knew no bounds.

For all three were wolves-heads, outlaws to a man and all sought shelter in the greenwoods that were Inglewood Forest.

The three loved their life in the wild wood, poaching deer and enjoying many adventures just like their kinsman Robin Hood. But William was a married man and he missed his wife Alice and their children. And so it was that one day he decided he would visit them where they lived in Carlisle, but Adam and Clim warned him not to go, saying, 'If thou art caught, William, your life will be at an end!' But William listened not, for such was his desire to make merry with his family that he would risk being slain.

With cloak, hood and a broad-brimmed hat serving as a disguise, William made his way to Carlisle and went straightaway to his house where Alice and the children's joy at seeing their husband and father was so great it could not be dampened by the knowledge that the justice had posted a watch upon William's house. He cuddled his children, he kissed and caressed his wife and ordered her to fetch meat and drink aplenty. 'For tonight,' said William, 'we shall be of good cheer!'

But there was another in this household, whom you have yet to meet – an old woman who had lived off the charity of Cloudesley and his family for many years. Her pleasure at seeing the outlaw returned home was alas of the self-serving sort. She made her excuses and went straightaway to the justice, where, upon the promise of a new gown and perhaps some coin, she told him that 'William of Cloudesley had come to Carlisle and rejoices with his family this night'. The justice went to the sheriff and told him all that the old crone had said and now both men went before their servants and officials and before other citizens of the town who were loyal to their harsh administration. They gathered all together and told them that they must make haste to the house of William Cloudesley, lest he disappear back to the greenwoods from whence he had come.

A great crowd surrounded William's house, but Alice was a woman like many in this book who spoke her mind and would have chided the Devil himself had he threatened her household. She cried 'treason!' saddened to see so many yeomen about the crowd, men who were no different to her husband in estate or degree, yet all too willing to serve corrupt rulers, for in doing so they also served themselves. She took up a poleaxe, while her husband William took up his sword, buckler and bow, both willing to die rather than be separated from each other again. William loosed arrow after arrow at the justice and the sheriff, but both were well armoured and his arrows broke upon the iron plate that covered their chests.

Still neither William nor Alice would yield and the justice ordered that their house be fired, that the family be burned alive. Flames soon flew high about the house, feasting upon the timber frame, yet its appetite was not easily sated and now it sought to dine upon human flesh. With woe in his heart William had no choice but to cast his family from a window, saving them, so that they might revenge themselves upon his enemies and now he loosed arrow after arrow until his back was scorched and his bowstring smouldered. The burnt and blackened outlaw leapt from the fire that longed to be his tomb and with sword and buckler held high, he ran thither and yon striking down any of the sheriff's men who came close and collecting the limbs of many of the justice's servants besides!

He hacked this way and slashed the other until his anger was spent and his enemies fell upon him. The outlaw William of Cloudesley, good yeoman that he was, was bound hand and foot and taken to Carlisle castle, there to await his terrible fate. The following day a new gallows was built in his honour and the town gates were all shut tight, for the sheriff and justice were taking no chances. 'This day,' said the justice to William, 'thou shalt be hanged and neither Clim of the Clough, Adam Bell, nor even the Devil from hell himself will save you!'

But the town swineherd, a boy who knew William well, heard that the brave outlaw was to be hanged. He had often met him in Inglewood, while he fattened his hogs upon acorns and nuts. The lad thought William a good man, who had given him food and helped him when in need. The boy was slight and so found a small crevice in the town walls where only he could pass through. Quickly he ran to the greenwoods, to the camp of Clim of the Clough and Adam Bell, and told them his dire dispatch, that William's neck was to be stretched that very day! 'Alas,' the good companions cried, 'that our brother is to die, but think we not this day!' And the outlaws mounted horses and made swift way to Carlisle.

The gates were barred against them, but this was no hurdle to two as artful as Adam and Clim. They pretended to be officers of the king and beguiled the porter within with talk of messages from their sovereign and a letter sealed by his royal hand, warning the dull-witted man that if he would not let them pass then he was 'a fool and would be hanged like a thief'. The man was truly a dolt, for he opened the gate and it was an evil opening for him as Clim wrung the man's neck and stole the keys from his belt.

Having secured their escape route, Adam and Clim strung their good yew bows and took to two sides of the marketplace where the newly built gallows stood. They could see the sheriff and justice standing over William their friend, as a man in their employ measured up Cloudesley for his grave. His fee was the clothes the good yeoman was to be hanged in, but Cloudesley had cast his eye about the market and seeing his friends watching from afar, his mood lifted. 'It is a wonder to some, but not me,' said he, 'that the man who measures me this day for my grave, will tomorrow be lying therein himself!' But the sheriff and justice took no notice, the justice vowing to hang William of Cloudesley with his own hand.

Those were the last words he was to speak for Adam Bell had him in his aim as his brother in outlawry, Clim, had the sheriff in his. Both outlaws fitted an arrow to their bow, both leant and shot, loosing their arrows at the same time, and never had two finer shots been seen in Carlisle, for both found their mark.

Both the sheriff and justice fell from their mounts, blood spilling from their death wounds as the people of Carlisle fled. All who stayed were deemed by the outlaws to be the supporters of the two dead officials and so enemies of the common man, whereby Clim and Adam felt no shame in loosing arrow after arrow at them all and striking them down with sword and axe whenever they came close. They cut William's bonds and he too with sword and bow threw many a man to the ground leaving their hearts cold, their eyes lifeless and their wives widows.

By the time they fought their way back to the dead porter's gate, three hundred of those who were loyal to sheriff and justice lay dead, but not the three brave outlaws who were out of the town and riding swiftly back to the greenwood. That night the whole of Carlisle was beset with wailing and grief, yet at the trysting tree where outlaws met in Inglewood all were making merry, eating and drinking their fill and enjoying good cheer. They had shown themselves to be doughty yeomen worthy of the tales long told about them, although as any who have ever heard me at my craft, telling tales, will surely know, stories grow in the telling and this tale still has a way to go before it ends.

Alice and her children came to Inglewood, for they had no other place to go and were wretched, thinking that William was dead. When at last they found each other there was much rejoicing between William and Alice, between husband and wife. William of Cloudesley, Adam Bell and Clim of the Clough took up their bows and each slew a fat hart and the family supped well that night. But the following day the three companions left early to seek a pardon from the King of England himself so that Alice and the children could rest easy once more. For after all, their quarrel was not with the king, but only those who governed cruelly in his name, those who abused their position and grew fat and rich on poor men's thin backs!

The ragged rugged outlaws went straightaway to London and were brought before the monarch. He listened as all three knelt before him and asked their sovereign lord's forgiveness.

'Sire,' they said, 'we are Adam Bell, Clim of the Clough and William of Cloudesley and we ask your forgiveness for that we have slain many of your fat fallow deer in many of your forests.' But the king knew well their names; he called them 'base-born thieves and pilfering poachers', and ordered that they be hanged for their crimes. But his queen took pity upon the three companions; perhaps she thought them honest men, or simply liked their lusty look! Whatever her reason she begged a favour of her husband the king, reminding him that 'when first we married you promised to grant me the first boon I asked. Well now dear husband,' said she, 'I ask you to release these men into my service.' The king had no choice, for he had sworn it upon his kingship and so he let the outlaws go. The three companions were washed and dressed in the queen's own livery and once more they made merry, eating and drinking their fill and enjoying good cheer.

But still this tale is not yet done, for messages arrived at the king's court telling him that in Carlisle a great wrong had been done. That the sheriff, the justice and three hundred of their men had been killed. He read from a letter sealed by survivors of the slaughter, stating that it was Adam Bell, Clim of the Clough and William of Cloudesley who had murdered the rulers of that city to say nothing of the forty foresters of the fee brutally slain and many a bailiff and beadle besides. The king was sorely grieved for he had sworn upon his kingship not to hang the three outlaws and there was nothing he could do to harm them, for he had more honour than those who lay dead in Carlisle.

Still he wanted recompense and so he summoned all three to an archery competition, challenging them all that they were no match for his best archers, for as the king said, 'I will see more of these outlaws who have wrought ruin in the north.' The king's men and the three companions shot at butts set at fifty paces and many hit the prick, the very heart of the target. This was no sport and the three outlaws grew bored. 'How would it be,' said William, 'that we leave these childish games behind. For instead of shooting at those great straw butts, I think we shoot at those thin hazel wands?' and he pointed to a field where hazel grew thickly.

The king agreed and hazel rods were stuck in the ground at twenty score paces, which is four hundred strides to all of you and me. The king thought that such a shot was impossible for a mortal man, but William of Cloudesley fitted arrow to bow, he leant, he aimed, he shot. The arrow was spat from the bow, it spun fast and cleft hard the hazel rod in two. 'Truly,' said the king, 'thou art the finest bowman I have ever seen.'

A lesser man would have thought his prowess well attested, but not Cloudesley. For next he claimed his skill was such that he could split an apple at six score paces, which is one hundred and twenty strides to all of you and me. Now some of you may be thinking that such a shot was not a great feat since he had already split a wand at four hundred paces, but you have not the knowledge to which I lay claim, for the apple was to be placed upon his own son's head! So think again, this was to be the hardest arrow William ever loosed, a shocking shot to all gathered there including the king who warned William of the consequences. 'If your arrow misses its mark this day,' said the king, 'if it but clips a hair on your son's head, then by all the saints in heaven I shall have you and your companions hanged this very hour!'

Cloudesley looked to Clym and Adam Bell and they nodded back. Six score paces were counted out, a stake was knocked into the ground and William's son was bound to it. William turned the boy's face away, so he would not flinch, and set the apple upon his head. He took his time, stroking the bow and whispering wondrous words. William of Cloudesley fitted arrow to bow, he leant, he aimed, he shot. The arrow was spat from the bow, it spun fast and cleft hard the apple in two.

The king saw the finest of all shots that day and knew in his heart that it was as well to have William shooting for him as against him. He offered the best of all archers eighteen pence a day, a fortune to a good yeoman, if he would 'bear the king's bow'. William agreed and was made chief ranger of all the north country, while Clim of the Clough and Adam Bell were appointed Yeomen of the King's Chamber and were paid twelve pence each a day for the privilege! Even Alice gained a position as chief gentlewoman of the queen's nursery. So you see in a story at least, three outlaws and an outlaw's wife gained authority and status in a royal court of England and so in a story at least, poor men and indeed poor women really did have their say!

OF THE KING AND THE RADISH

T he mayor of any Tudor city was the representative of the monarch; he was in effect his or her equal in the great urban centres. Rich and powerful and yet still they were openly attacked by men like Thomas Benson, a cobbler who was ordered to give sureties of his good behaviour because 'he bid a turd in the Mayor's teeth and wished him out of office so he could sue the Mayor'. Also George King, who was committed to prison for 'misbehaving of himself in the face of the court with stout words towards Mr Mayor'. Another wealthier citizen of Norwich, Robert Allen, was also 'committed to ward [prison] there to remain with a block on his leg and to lye in the free chamber and not the jailor's house', for having written a slanderous letter against the mayor, Robert Suckling. That he was to be held in the free chamber and not in the jailer's house is an important distinction. At this time a man of means who was imprisoned could pay to stay in relative luxury in comfortable cells and even in the jailer's house, but Suckling was so offended by Allen's slander that he didn't want him to enjoy his time inside!

Men of means like Allen and even a poor fellow like Benson were more than happy to criticise their rulers and they enjoyed tales where lowborn heroes did just that. Although not necessarily stories where they fell foul of their rulers, but rather comic gests and moral tales where they could become a monarch's equal and teach him something of a life hard lived ...

Long ago in far-off France there lived a king brought low by the lies and conspiracies that ran rampant in his court. He was surrounded on all sides by grovelling courtiers who played the king and each other false and were only out to take what estates and power they could. The games of state they played were always at the expense of others, including their ruler.

All his life the king had been raised to rule, to know no other way except telling others what to do, to live off the backs of his people and deal with creeping, crawling courtiers, so called noblemen who would quite happily see him fall and fight among themselves over who should take his place. But all his life the king had thought that there was a better way to live, a life free of intrigue and pomp. He longed to deal no more with ambassadors from foreign lands, many of whom would be happy to see him fall and then fight among themselves over whose king from a far off land should take his place!

The king's realm was troubled by war and this troubled him greatly. Whether it be war with other realms or war within his domain, such were the king's woes that he no longer slept and instead lay awake longing for a life less ordered. He ate little and ailed much, for he was so tired in both mind and body that he fell ill. The finest doctors of physic, well known apothecaries, and even the odd low-born barber surgeon were brought to the court and ordered to heal the king upon pain of death, but none could cure his affliction. The doctors stared long and hard at the king's urine, the apothecaries all muttered of an imbalance of his humours that made him melancholic, while the surgeons talked only of bleeding and purging the king of what little strength he had left!

None could cure the king; instead, their services only served to make him feel worse. The only respite he had from the attentions of fawning courtiers and quack doctors was when he went out riding with the hunt. It was not the slaying of innocent animals, you understand, for the king had seen far too much killing done in his name already. Instead, the king thought of it as time to escape the court and the dull, dreary men in their fine fancy clothes. It was a time when he felt free, although the knowledge that he must return to the court always lay heavy upon him.

But one day while out hunting, the king's horse threw a shoe and he was left alone on the edge of a wood. Not knowing where he was, or where his servants had gone, the king led his horse across the fields until he came to the house of a husbandman, a poor man who made his living tilling the soil and growing only that which he needed to feed his family. Growing peas, beans, onions and radishes, the surplus was sold to buy wool for clothes and grain for bread and beer. Whatever else he needed, from wood for the fire to meat for the table, was taken from the nearby woods. His was a simple life, free of conspiracy. The poor man was far more concerned with putting food on the table to feed his family than with plotting to overthrow his neighbours and take their land!

And so it was that the king found peace in the company of the poor man and his family. He asked them if he might stay a while so that he too would know the simple happiness and plain truth of a plain and simple life. The husbandman was glad to have him, for another pair of hands would not go amiss when there was so much that needed doing. The king exchanged his fine and fancy gown for plain and simple clothes. He ploughed the field with the husbandman and when the crops began to grow, he weeded with the husbandman's wife and scared the birds away with his children. He rose early and trapped coneys and other small game, which he helped the husbandman's wife prepare for the pot. He tended the fire and mended his own plain and simple clothes and when the day's work was done he would sit by the husbandman taking in the beauty of the world about them – looking out over fine fields, fair forest and a gently flowing stream. And then as night fell he would join the whole family as they feasted upon all that they had grown and all that they had caught. A small feast yes, but a tasty meal just the same. In fact, the king had never eaten food as fine as this; his favourite were the radishes, for he had grown them with his own hand and as anyone who has ever grown a radish will know, they always taste so much better when you have grown them yourself!

For a whole year the king lived a plain, simple and honest life tilling the soil, doing only that which he needed to survive. It was hard work and he heard tell from the husbandman how a poor harvest could blight a poor family's life. His body and heart ached from hard work and tales of hard times, but hidden away as he was from the conspiracies of court he had grown happy and healthy, although his realm alas had not. For long ago a realm without a king could be an unhappy place, not least because the not-so-noble courtiers were fighting among themselves over who should rule in his stead. His realm was falling into ruin, for war was upon the land and soon it would reach the farm where the king had found refuge from all his woes. With a heavy heart he thanked the husbandman and his family for all their many kindnesses and he left, riding his horse back to the stink of the city and the court that was fouler still.

The king took charge once again and when the government of his land was restored, he settled back down to a life of luxury and lies. In time he grew used to it again and forgot about the plain and simple honest pleasures that could be had from tilling the soil and making do. He buried himself in matters of state and thought no more of the land.

A year went by and on the small farm the husbandman missed his friend the king, for he had been a great help and good company. And so it was, his wife counselled the husbandman to pay a visit to his friend at his palace and by way of a gift, take him some of the radishes that the king had enjoyed so much while he had lived and worked on their small farm. 'Give the king these roots,' she said, 'to remind him of the good cheer he had when he made our house his home.' But her husband thought she was mad. He told her so, saying 'a great king such as would not remember such plain and simple pleasures'. He may have thought his wife mad, but the woman would not rest until her husband had taken up a great bunch of their finest radish roots and set off on his journey towards the stink of the city and the even fouler court.

The road was long, the journey hard and the poor husbandman was forced to eat all but one of the radishes meant for the king. He waited many days lined up with other poor people of the realm, all trying to glimpse the king as he was processed from one place to another and with any amount of circumstance and much pomp besides. But for all the ceremony and celebration the king stared blankly out across the waiting crowds until he saw his friend the husbandman and had him brought over.

The poor man was shown to the king's great halls and now he stood before the ruler and his courtiers, all of whom looked down upon the man who was clearly so much lower born than they. They sneered as the husbandman presented his friend the king with a gift wrapped in a piece of plain and simple cloth.

The king did not sneer or look down upon his friend. Opening the cloth he saw the single radish and was straightaway taken back to the time when he had found happiness and health tilling the soil; to a time when he had found a simple truth doing only those things he needed to survive; tending the fire and mending his own plain and simple clothes; sitting by the husbandman and taking in the beauty of the world about them; looking out over fine fields, fair forest and a gently flowing stream and feasting with the whole family. A small feast yes, but all tasted good. In fact, the king had never eaten food as fine as he had the year he tilled the soil. His favourite were the radishes, for he had grown them with his own hand and as anyone who has ever grown a radish will know, they always taste so much better when you have grown them yourself!

Once more the king felt free. That solitary radish had brought back good memories that he swore he would never lose again. He had the radish set among the finest jewels in his strongroom and now he thought, 'I am king and so for such a wonderful gift from my friend the poor husbandman, it is required of me that I give him an equally wonderful reward, but what?' And so it was that he ordered his servants to pay the poor husbandman a thousand gold coins, one fine gift for another. The king's noblemen and courtiers thought him mad, but there was one who above all others saw opportunity in all situations. He was a pickthank, a flatterer of kings; that is perhaps why he was most powerful of all the nobles. It was he who had the king's ear and much of the land to boot. He was a rich and powerful man, who craved greater riches still. When he saw that the king had paid a poor man a thousand gold coins for one radish, he grew jealous. 'That's not right,' he said; 'that's not fair.' But then he thought, 'Hold on, wait a minute. If the king gave the poor man a thousand gold coins for one radish, then what riches would he give me for my finest white charger, my finest white horse?' And so it was, the rich nobleman gave his best horse to the king.

The king was very pleased, for he had never been given such a fair and fine horse before. He thought, 'I am king and so for such a wonderful gift it is required of me that I must give the nobleman an equally wonderful reward. But what?' He set to thinking and soon he thought of the finest of gifts for the most powerful of all his courtiers. He sent it to the man in a beautiful box, finely carved it was and with cunningly wrought hinges and lock. It was handed to the not-so-noble nobleman right there in the king's halls and he fair shook thinking of all the gold and perhaps even jewels held within. All watched as the fawning fellow took up the key and turned it in the lock. All held their breath and said nothing as the creeping courtier slowly, oh so very slowly, lifted the lid.

But as he did, the smile fell from his face as water falls from a duck's back, for in that beautiful decorated box there was a plain and simple radish! The king had given the courtier a treasure worth a thousand gold coins, but a gift far more valuable still to those who knew both the pleasure and the pain of tilling the soil.

OF THE VILLAGE OF FOOLS

This story is adapted from a collection of tales entitled *The Wise Men of Gotham* and although it was not printed until around 1630, there is plenty of evidence that some of the stories were already popular a century earlier. Will Kemp, a famous Tudor player, had previously performed one episode in the 1630 edition on stage while another two stories were adapted from versions in *The Hundred Merry Tales*, published in 1526.

The tale is included here because it tells of King John, a much-hated monarch whose subjects rebelled against him. It's important to remember that many of the Tudor poor who did speak their minds were not calling for the right to rule themselves: such ideas were not really voiced until the Civil War of the following century. Rather, what concerned them most was ending corruption, lowering prices and protecting their long-held common rights, whether it be from the nobility or the oligarchies that ran the great cities long ago. That's why John Cobbe, a weaver, was put in the cage for 'speaking seditious words against engrosses of corn'. In other words, for speaking out against the greed of rich men, who were keeping hold of corn meant for the poor and driving the prices up.

I think that's why the story was so popular in Tudor England, because when 'bad King John' was forced into agreeing to the Magna Carta several hundred years before, it was not so much a rebellion against a king, rather a revolt against bad kingship. The rebels only wanted to reform John, a desire to teach him a lesson that held true for most in the sixteenth century, hence the popularity of stories like the one below.

That said, the cultural historian Margaret Spufford believed that stories such as this appealed mainly to a sophisticated urban readership who enjoyed tales about quaint country bumpkins.[18] I disagree; yes we can laugh at the foolishness of the characters set below, but there is wisdom in their madness, which, as you will see, allowed them to get the better of their betters …

There was once a king called John. Horrible King John some called him, while others called him Bad King John, and as for those who did not have the courage of their convictions, they just called him Not Very Nice King John. Most people long ago did not like John and his superior London ways, especially when he brought those ways to where they lived!

For one day word reached the poor folk of the village of Gotham that King John wanted to build a hunting lodge in woodland near their homes. The good people of that village flew into a panic, fearing that they would lose all rights to deer and wild boar. 'Oh no,' they cried, 'if Bad King John hunts our land, then we won't be able to hunt. For if we are caught hunting our land, when Bad King John is hunting our land, he will surely cut off our hands or pluck out our eyes. He might even hang us until we are dead!' And so the good people of Gotham came together in their church. They talked and they talked and they talked some more, until at last they had made a plan and now they waited for the king's men to come.

The villagers did not have to wait too long, for a few days later the king's herald, the king's messenger, rode into the village of Gotham. As the herald rode into the village he peered all about him, looking for the good people of Gotham, but of the villagers there was no sign. This was very strange, for normally when the herald and his men rode into a village, its people would run from their houses to gaze upon the finely dressed men mounted on their finely dressed horses. But this village was quiet; there was no one around.

And so it was that the herald continued riding through the village until he got to the pond where he met a girl who was crying loudly, while tears spilt down her face and dripped into the very edge of the water. Such were her tears that the herald was moved and asked the child what ailed her? The girl spoke. 'It's the moon,' she cried, 'the moon has fallen from the heavens and drowned!' And now the girl told the herald how just last night she had been walking past the pond and had seen the moon floating in the water. 'I tried to save her,' she said, 'I tried to pull her out with my mother's distaff, but I couldn't and now the moon has sunk beneath the water. She is drowned!' Once more the girl fell to sobbing, her whole body shaking as the herald shook his head. For he had travelled the length and breadth of England and witnessed many strange and wondrous things, but he had never met any as foolish as this child before. 'This girl is clearly mad,' he said, 'she is such a halfwit and a ninny-hammer that we had best be on our way.'

But no sooner had the herald turned his horse than he heard a door slam and a man in naught but his naked shirt came running down the street clutching a writhing, wriggling eel in his hands. The man leapt into the pond and held the eel beneath the water. The herald looked at the man standing up to his knees in the pond and asked him his business? The half naked fellow spoke. 'This here fish is a bad fish. This here fish is a greedy fish, for it ate all the other fish in the river,' he said, 'and so we have decided to punish this fish by drowning it in this here pond!' The old man shook with rage, thinking of all the fish the greedy eel had eaten, while the herald shook his head. For he had travelled the length and breadth of England and witnessed many strange and wondrous things, but he had never met any as foolish as this fellow before. 'This man is clearly mad,' he said, 'he is such a halfwit and a ninny-hammer that we had best be on our way.'

Once more the herald and his men began riding through the village of Gotham, but they hadn't gone very far when they met an old man riding upon an even older horse. He was riding upon a horse, yet still he carried a heavy sack of grain upon his back. So heavy was the sack upon the man's back that he was forced to lean over his horse's neck as he rode along and the herald asked him why he struggled so? He asked the old man why he didn't just lay the heavy sack across the horse's back so that he didn't have to carry it? But the old man looked at the herald as if he were mad and then he spoke. 'I would not be so cruel,' he said, 'for my horse is very old, my horse is very tired and so I carry the sack so the poor old horse doesn't have to!' The old man continued on his way his frail old body shaking beneath the weight of the sack, while the herald shook his head. For he had travelled the length and breadth of England and witnessed many strange and wondrous things, but he had never met any as foolish as this codger before. 'This old man is clearly mad,' he said, 'he is such a halfwit and a ninny-hammer that we had best be on our way.'

The herald and his men picked up their pace, but now they were slowed by a fast-moving river where twelve men stood at the water's edge sobbing. The louder the cries of the one, the louder the replies of the others and so surprised was the herald to see twelve full-grown men weeping that he asked them all what it could be that had brought them so low? The tallest one among them spoke. 'This very day we twelve friends went fishing here at the river, but now only eleven of us remain.' The tallest man counted the others standing before him, but did not count himself. 'You see,' said he, 'one of us has gone missing this day and like the moon, is surely drowned!' Once more the fishermen fell into grief, their bodies shaking as the herald shook his head. For he had travelled the length and breadth of England and witnessed many strange and wondrous things, but he had never met any as foolish as this lot before. 'These men are clearly mad,' he said, 'they are such halfwits and ninny-hammers that we had best be on our way.'

Alas for the herald he had not gone far when he met many of the men, many of the women and many of the children of Gotham, all coming the other way and all carrying great bundles of heavy wood in their arms. They were huffing and puffing beneath their loads, yet were merry in their work and the herald, dismounting from his horse, was curious to know why all were so joyous? What had lifted them so high this day? The oldest among them, an ancient women, spoke. 'Herald,' said she, 'herald,' she said, 'do you see that great field yonder?' The herald looked and he saw a wide open field. 'Herald,' said she, 'herald,' she said, 'do you see in that field there stands a tall, tall tree?' The herald looked and he saw a great oak tree. 'Herald,' said she, 'herald,' she said, 'do you see in that tree that there is a cuckoo bird?' The herald looked and he saw a cuckoo nesting in the oak. 'Herald,' said she, 'herald,' she said, 'so pretty is its call and so fine are its feathers that we mean to build a fence about the tree so that we can pen that bird and can keep it for our own!'

The good people of Gotham set to work building the fence and when it was done they danced about the cuckoo in its tree, twirling this way and leaping the other, while the herald leapt back on to his horse. For he had travelled the length and breadth of England and witnessed many strange and wondrous things, but he had never met any as foolish as the odd folk of Gotham before. 'These people are clearly mad,' he said, 'they are all so cuckoo that we had best be on our way!'

The herald galloped quickly out of the village, but saw many other strange goings-on before he was finally free of folly. From the halfwit who ran across a field and leapt into his hose, to the old dolt who hauled her cow up onto the roof of her house. From the ninny-hammer who rode upon a three-legged stool, to the dullards who sent their cheeses off to market to sell themselves! Such stupidity only served to spur the herald on and when at last he returned to London, he went straightaway to the palace of King John. 'John,' he said, for he knew the king very well. 'Do not go hunting near the village of Gotham, for they are a village of fools!' And so it was that Bad King John never ever went hunting near that village and the good people of Gotham kept their boar and their deer for their own. For while they were a village of fools, there was much wisdom and even more cleverness in their madness!

OF THE VILLAGE WHERE
INSULTS FLOWED FREELY

In the year 1600, a man called Rumbold was found guilty of bribing Cicily Foukard with a 'russet cloth' if she would but say in open market that Wragg had 'attempted her chastity', while in the same year, Ann Shering appeared before the mayor's court and 'did openly ask Roger Watson forgiveness for that she had maliciously and falsely slandered him saying that he would have ravished her [and that] she did it of devilish intent to take away his good name'. Such was the power of insults and slanders, especially of a sexual nature, that false allegations like these were common and seen as an ideal way of attacking an enemy, by attacking his or her reputation.

When John Reeve slandered Edmund Prettye, Prettye said that the slander 'impaired a man's credit', and also, 'for a man that would live in good estimation would not have his name touched with any such reports'. He also told a witness that 'he would undertake great cost' to preserve it.

Credit was everything to Tudor men, for it referred to both their economic situation and wider social and political status. The two were inexorably entwined, for a man's wealth or lack thereof dictated his standing in the wider world, which is why when poor men appeared as witnesses in Tudor court cases, they were often described as being men of 'light credit'. William Sanderson, for example, was described as having no credit because he was 'a poor man who liveth yearly by his labours'. There was also William Rudd who was described as 'a very lewd person of life and conversation', and was therefore considered to be 'of little or no credit or estimation'. The implication was that his poverty was the result of his own foolishness and other failings in his character and he was therefore not to be trusted. But then again, credit and wit takes many forms …

There was once a man of noble birth who, like many from his time and a lot from ours, looked down upon those who had not enjoyed the benefits that a purse full of coin can bring. He thought all poor men and women were naught but witless fools. Like many of his age, he thought they were people of little credit, lacking in both means and character. Indeed, like many long ago he thought that the poor deserved to be poor, because they did not have the wit to raise themselves up above their lowly station in life.

Then as now there were some whose views were blinkered by a closeted upbringing, where status, education and privilege served only to limit their view of the world about them. And so it was with our man of noble birth, until one day having lost his way, he rode his horse into a certain village. Where it was I do not know, but you may picture this tale where it pleases you most.

Our man of noble birth had not gone far when he met a courtier, a high-born man much like himself and after introductions they rode a while together. They passed by a young carter with his back to them both. He was rough in both complexion and dress and so the courtier mocked the carter calling him rude and saying that he had need of a mirror to dress by. The carter, though, perceived the jest and returned it twofold: 'Why sir,' said he, 'I have no need of a mirror for I have a wall eye, that looks where it will and when I use it to look over my shoulder, I see a knave looking back at me!' Our man of noble birth laughed loudly at the carter's wit and continued without the courtier who, shame-faced and not laughing, took another road.

Our nobleman rode on, trotting past a cordwainer, a shoemaker about his business; having never seen the craft before he decided to tarry a while, to linger so that he might know more of the art. But as our rich man marvelled at the cobbler's skill with leather, thread and nail, a miner passed by. Black he was from a day's digging in the earth and so the shoemaker mocked him, calling the miner a demon from hell, asking of news from that fiery place and of the health of his master, the Devil. The miner, though, perceived the jest and returned it twofold: 'Why friend,' said he, 'the Devil fares well, for when last we met he was happy knowing that soon he would have a cobbler come to his domain to mend his boots!' Our man of noble birth laughed louder still, enjoying the skilled hands of the one man and the wit of the other. The shoemaker though said naught, and set his gaze to the half-stitched boot upon his knee.

Our rich man was enjoying his journey, for it was a long time since he had laughed so heartily. Laughing still, he saw a schoolteacher with a book in his hands and face to the heavens, studying the sky, he was asking how and why? Such was his devotion to his studies that he did not see the ditch in front of him and now the master fell arse over elbow, dropping his book upon the muddy track. Our nobleman went to assist, but was beaten to it by an old woman of the village who helped him up, although the teacher, feeling foolish, mocked her, saying that one so lowly as she could not raise him up on high. The old woman, though, perceived the jest and returned it twofold:

'Why master,' said she, 'while it is true that I know nothing of the heavens above, I do have the sense to see that which is beneath my feet and it was not I who fell from grace this day!' Once more our nobleman laughed lustily, while the old women went happily one way, the teacher the other. Although whether he too were smiling I cannot say, for his head hung lower than ever it had before.

Having rode on a short while, our nobleman crossed a ford in the stream that wandered about the village and there he saw a young maid stooping down by the edge of the water, washing her clothes. As she bent low her tight smock was drawn between her buttocks and a friar who was passing close by saw what our rich man saw and mocked the young woman, saying that her horse was biting hard upon his bridle. The young maid, though, perceived the jest and returned it twofold. 'Why good brother,' said she, 'he is not biting his bit, but only wiping his mouth so that you might come and kiss it!' Scowling at the lashing he had received from the wise maid's tongue, the friar leapt the ford and went quickly on his way, while our man of noble birth smiled broadly and continued on his.

Our nobleman had laughed himself hungry and so aimed his horse towards an inn of the village that had brought him so much gladness. Drawing close he saw another rich man who looked down on all those who could not match his wealth and status. The other alighted from his fine horse and ordered a poor boy to hold the reins of his mount while he went inside to eat his fill. He offered the boy no coin for his services and instead mocked the lad saying that a base-born boy such as he and a tethering post had much in common. The poor boy, though, perceived the jest and returned it twofold: 'Why sir,' said the boy, 'this is a sturdy fierce horse, so can one so slight be sure to hold him?' The rich man, impatient for a feast, replied, 'Yes, he is a calm beast and even a weak fellow may hold him well enough.' 'Well,' said the lad, 'if that be true sir, then I pray you hold the horse yourself!' The lad ran away, giggling as he went while the other rich man laughed not. With a face like thunder he sought another to hold his horse. He went into the inn closely followed by our nobleman who enjoyed the poor lad's wit as much as he enjoyed the bread and capons that were set before him that day.

As our rich man ate his fill he listened to the conversation betwixt two others, a wealthy merchant and a miller. The merchant thought that all millers were greedy to a man and so he mocked him, saying that good, honest millers were well known for having golden thumbs, and yet he did not have one. The miller, though, perceived the jest and returned it twofold: 'Why friend,' said he, 'in truth my thumb is gold, but such are its properties that a man who has been made cuckold by an unfaithful wife cannot see it!' The merchant left without finishing his meal; while our nobleman could not easily finish his food, for so great was his laughter that he could scarce find time to swallow!

But finish his feast our man did and he was just mopping his plate when he saw hidden in a dark corner a yeoman and his wife who had fallen into arguing, the yeoman's mood made all the worse by a sore tooth that ached mercilessly and also by his wife's failing concern. Seeing the women's lack of care, her husband mocked her mercilessly saying that his tooth grieved him so sore he wished it were in her backside instead. His wife, though, perceived the jest and returned it twofold: 'Why husband,' said she, 'if your tooth were in my tail it would do little good, but if there were anything between my cheeks that could heal your tooth, I wish it were in your mouth right now!' At her words the husband shut his mouth, not least because his tooth still ached and because he knew that he had been bested.

You might think that the goodwife's words put our nobleman off his food, but they did not. Instead her reply was the sweet pudding to a feast of wit that had filled him with great cheer that day. Not even the juiciest of tarts could have pleased him so much as that woman's clever tongue had done. And so it was, filled with fine food and even greater joy, our man of noble birth rode out of the village where insults flowed freely and back to the great houses and good people who lived within. He told them all the stories that I have just told to you and suggested to all those high-born lords and ladies that what the low-born folk lacked in wealth, they made up for in wit. He said it was a rude wit, yes, but wit just the same. 'Perhaps,' said our man of noble birth, 'we should think of it as wisdom in the rough!'

CHAPTER V

A CAVEAT FOR COMMON CURSITORS

OF THE MILLER WHO STOLE THE NUTS

In 1566 Thomas Harman wrote *A Caveat or Warning for Common Cursetors*, in which he listed the various types of villain and rogue and also 'cant speak', the secret language of the Elizabethan underworld. He wrote of Priggers of Prancers, meaning horse thieves, and also 'rufflers', former soldiers who had taken to a life of vagabondage. There were also 'hookers', who used iron hooks attached to long poles to steal from open windows, and 'dummerers', who feigned being mute to con the charitable into giving them alms. Harman also wrote of 'nipping a bung', meaning to steal a purse, to cut the strings that attached it to its owner's belt, a common form of theft in Tudor England.[19]

Thieves started at an early age and a letter from William Fleetwood, the Recorder of London, to Lord Burghley, written in 1585, tells of a school of pickpockets; of a certain gentleman who had fallen on hard times and set up an alehouse where he also trained young boys to be 'foists' (pickpockets) and 'nippers' (cutpurses). The gentleman would hang up a purse with hawk bells about it and 'he that could take out a counter without any noise was allowed to be a public foister: and he that could take a piece of silver out of the purse without the noise of any of the bells, was adjudged a judicial nipper'.[20]

Cutting purses was easily done on crowded urban markets and village fairs, but when caught, the thief could expect to be dealt with swiftly, although not always that harshly. Thus when John Frettisham was found guilty of stealing some sayes, a type of cloth, he was set in the stocks with cloth hanging about his neck; the cloth was to detail his crime. Some wore papers on their heads with their crime written on it, but as many could not read items were frequently hung about the wrongdoer's neck. When Swayne's wife admitted to stealing, cooking and eating a goose, she was set in the stocks with a goose about her neck!

Others thieves made a living by abusing their position, including Mary Harrys who was released from jail on the charity of her master, Richard Cooke, a worsted weaver, but then she absconded with his best linen. It was probably because this was not her first offence, coupled with the fact that she had stolen from her own master, that resulted in her much harsher punishment, for it was ordered that she be whipped about the market.

In the late sixteenth century, a combination of poor harvests and high prices saw a rise in crime and consequently, much harsher treatments as that dealt out to Mary Harrys, but then as now, many stole out of need to feed their families. It was a way of life for some in the great Tudor towns and cities and also in many stories like this one. A tale of theft and wrongdoing, but also a farce; of mistaken identity and misunderstanding – themes worthy of a Shakespearian comedy, even if my prose is not ...

There was once a farmer who really loved nuts. Such was his pleasure that he planted many a filbert tree in his orchard and he tended them carefully all his life. Such was his pleasure that when he died, he had a great sack of them buried with him in the ground to take on to the next world. Well, it just so happened that the local miller, a man famed for the wearing of a white coat, also had a passion for nuts. And so it was, on the night of the day that the farmer was buried, he decided to steal some of the dead man's crop for himself. On the way he met his friend the tailor who was famed for the wearing of a black coat. The tailor having no love of nuts had decided instead to steal one of the dead farmer's sheep.

The two friends went about their bad business thieving the dead man's goods, the miller filching the nuts, the tailor mitching a sheep and by way of celebration they decided that they would meet back at the church porch. 'Whosoever arrives there first will wait for the other,' said the miller, 'and then we'll away to my mill for a nice bit of roast mutton and some sugared filberts for afters!' Well, both went a mitching, the miller stealing the nuts, the tailor stealing a sheep and as it happened it was the miller who was first to arrive back at the church porch. While he waited for the tailor, he decided he would crack and eat some of his ill-gotten gains.

But it was nine of the clock at night and time for the sexton who cared for the church to lock it up for the night. The sexton, a man of a nervous disposition, walked across the graveyard and as he did he heard a strange tap, tap, tapping and crack,

crack, cracking coming from the church. And peering into the dark porch he saw a figure all dressed in white, cracking and eating nuts. The sexton screamed inwardly, for to scream outwardly would have wakened the dead and he was already frightened enough. He knew this apparition must be the ghost of the farmer, risen from the grave in search of more nuts to eat! He ran quickly home and told his ancient father all that he had seen and all that he had heard. The old man did not believe his son and wished to see it for himself, but he was lame and could not walk and so he asked his son the sexton to carry him. The two set off towards the church, the son carrying the father upon his back.

The miller was still crack, crack, cracking and eating nuts in the church porch when looking up he saw a figure walking towards him carrying something heavy upon his back. Thinking it was his friend the tailor carrying a stolen sheep, he called out to him 'I hope that fellow upon your back is good and fat, for I've a need of some meat to balance all these nuts I've eaten this night.' Well, the sexton, hearing the miller's words and believing them to be from the ghost of the farmer, he cast his father down upon the road. 'Fat or lean,' yelled the sexton pointing to the old man, 'you can have him, but you won't have me.' The sexton ran away leaving his ancient father upon the road, but the old man he leapt up and he too ran away, as fast if not faster than his son.

Now the miller, seeing two men running the one after the other, he thought it must surely be someone chasing his friend the tailor, that someone had caught him stealing the sheep. 'Oh no,' he thought. 'If the tailor is caught he is sure to blab. He is sure to tell how I have stolen all these nuts.' And so it was the miller ran away leaving the filched sack of filberts behind. It was only a short while later that the tailor returned to the church porch carrying a stolen sheep that wriggled and squirmed upon his back. Seeing the half-eaten sack of nuts he knew that something must be wrong. 'The miller must be in trouble,' he thought, and so he decided to go to the miller's mill, for that was where the miller was sure to go.

Meanwhile the sexton's father had run back home, but the sexton ran to the house of the village priest. He told the man of God all that he had seen and all that he had heard. 'It's the farmer,' said the sexton. 'The farmer has risen from the grave and now he wanders abroad cracking nuts and seeking out the flesh of innocent men to eat!' The priest, like the sexton, was a man of a nervous disposition, but he was also a man of the cloth and knew what must be done. He would exorcise the ghost of the farmer. He would put an end to the unholy eating of nuts! And so it was the priest put on his whitest, cleanest surplice and other holy garb and he set out on the road to the churchyard, followed closely by the sexton.

The two men walked up the very road that the tailor was walking down and the tailor, seeing a man dressed all in white, he thought it was the miller. He called out to him, 'by God I have him. I have him firmly in my grasp,' meaning the sheep he carried upon his back. But the priest seeing a figure dressed all in black with something white that was a wriggling and squirming upon his back, he thought that it must be the Devil himself carrying the ghost of the farmer. That it must be Old Hob himself come to take the farmer to hell! The priest screamed inwardly, for to scream outwardly would have wakened the dead and he was already frightened enough. He ran away leaving the sexton standing upon the road, but the sexton, he too ran away, as fast if not faster than the priest.

Now the tailor, seeing two men running, the one after the other, he thought it must surely be someone chasing his friend the miller, that someone had caught him stealing the nuts. 'Oh no,' he thought. 'If the miller is caught he is sure to blab. He is sure to tell how I have stolen this sheep.' And so it was, the tailor ran towards the miller's mill, for that was where the miller was sure to go. But when the tailor arrived at the mill it was in darkness and the door was bolted against him. He beat upon the door calling out 'let me in for I have him firmly tied by the legs,' meaning the sheep he had tied fast upon his back. But the miller hiding within thought it was a constable calling out and that he had the tailor bound well with rope. The constable must have caught the tailor and now he had come for him! The miller ran screaming from the back door of his mill. He ran screaming down the very road that the priest and the sexton were running up. The two thought that the one all dressed in white must be the ghost of the farmer. He had escaped from the Devil and now he was after them! The sexton ran away, while the priest jumped into a ditch, but the ditch was deep and full of water. He called out, 'Help, help, help. For God's sake help!'

The tailor, meanwhile, having heard the back door of the mill slam shut, he ran around the side of the mill and saw the miller running one way and the sexton running another. He heard the priest calling, 'Help, help, help! For God's sake help!' He thought that it must be a constable with the watchmen from the village. They had caught the miller fair and square and now they would surely catch him! And so it was the tailor also ran away.

Picture the scene if you will. The tailor running here, the miller running there, the sexton running everywhere, while the priest cries out, 'Help, help, help! For God's sake help!' And if you can see in your mind's eye what I saw that night, the night of the day that they buried the farmer, well, you will surely think that all of them, that each and every one of them, was completely and utterly NUTS!

OF HOWLEGLAS AND THE CEILING
CUNNINGLY PAINTED

heft, like that seen in the last story, was common-place, but there were many other ways of relieving a person of their coin long ago. All kinds of con men and women plied their trades in Tudor England, travelling the land and beguiling the gullible, wherever they went. Men like William Denny, who was whipped for 'using slight of hand'. And John Allen, whipped for 'making men believe he could find things that were lost'. Also Ann Heynes, 'a fortune teller to be whipped at the post and set to work at the Bridewell'. Tricksters like Heynes were so common that they get a mention in an Elizabethan Act for the control of rogues and vagabonds: 'All idle persons ... feigning themselves to have knowledge in physiognomy, palmistry or other like crafty science, or pretending that they can tell destinies, fortunes or such other fantastical imaginations ... shall be taken adjudged and deemed rogues vagabonds and sturdy beggars and shall sustain such pain and punishment as by this Act is in that behalf appointed.'[21]

In truth tricksters would prey upon anyone, happily stealing a penny as much as a pound. 'Coney catchers', or con men as they later became known, often picked out naive looking people whom they termed 'coneys', the slang for a gullible rustic type. An innocent, easily conned at cards or by means of some other cunning ruse.

That said, stories about tricksters were very popular in Elizabethan England; Robin Hood, for example, often went abroad in disguise, deceiving those he met upon the path, while Casper Spanagle, a man described as a 'high German', was 'given leave to make show a motion [play] called *Slight of Hand* at the Angel', a tavern in Norwich.

Tricksters were also popular in sixteenth-century Germany and the most famous one of all was Til Eulenspiegal, whose stories were first printed in Germany around 1510. The stories are part of a much older oral tradition, and were soon translated into English where Eulenspiegal became Howleglas, who like his German counterpart was descended from Marolfus, a mythical twelfth-century jester of Solomon's court. As demand for their stories grew, they absorbed earlier trickster tales from around the world, just as their stories would later be absorbed and reworked into fairy tales. The story below is not that dissimilar to Hans Christian Andersen's nineteenth-century tale 'The Emperor's New Clothes'. I've chosen to tell it here, because Howleglas practises his art upon the rich, foolish and greedy and that is why I think he was so popular in Tudor times. For as Master Shakespeare writes in his *Measure for Measure*, 'O heaven! The vanity of wretched fools!'[22]

There was once a trickster, a beguiler of the foolish, a coney-catching cunning man called Howleglas who travelled from town to town, village to village and house to house, wearing many different disguises. Sometimes a priest, sometimes a potter, sometimes a pedlar of wares, but on this day he arrived in a city disguised as a painter. He went abroad boasting to all who would listen that he was the finest artist in all the land and that he had painted princes in portraits, ladies in landscapes and all manner of fair and fine folk in frescoes!

Such was the new-found fame of the master mountebank that his boasts reached the ears of the mayor, a man desperate to record his own fame and great credit in pigment and paint. And so it was, he sent for Howleglas and asked for his help. The aspiring artist gladly came to the mayor's fine house, eyeing the silver upon a cupboard in the hall, set there for all to see. One look and Howleglas could tell that here was a man who was desperate for all to know that he had arrived and what was more he was planning on staying put! Howleglas perceived the mayor to be a vain man who wanted everyone to know that he had earned his place upon high, although the mayor should have seen that vanity would bring him low. Alas he did not and so Howleglas told the foolish fellow that he would gladly paint his likeness, but suggested a greater project still, not upon canvas, nor wooden boards for that matter, but upon the ceiling instead. 'A fresco,' said Howleglas, 'in the latest Italian fashion, with you depicted upon a throne on high and with Dame Fame blowing her trumpet in your honour, surrounded by the great and the good of your city and all of you looking down upon everyone else!'

Well, all the talk of far-flung places and being enthroned in the firmament of his vaulting was too much for the mayor, and he felt sure that if he were set up high in heaven then none could pull him down. He agreed and the deal was sealed with a handshake and the promise of three hundred crowns for the work, one hundred of which was to be paid to Howleglas in advance for paint and labouring men's wages. He swore not to disturb the artist in his labours, nor trouble him until the work was complete. The bargain made, Howleglas sent for three men of his acquaintance, well-known fellows of little credit whom he set to work making merry, playing at dice and cards and behaving in a lewd and idle manner. Their only responsibility was that they should not betray him to the mayor or any other man, and now Howleglas, the master con man if not the master painter, had a scaffold built in the mayor's hall. While his men looked on, the cunning fellow hung great sheets across the ceiling so that none could see his art, for in truth there was no art to see! Not one stroke of the paintbrush was made as Howleglas set to playing with his boon companions, making merry, playing at dice and cards and behaving in a lewd and idle manner.

Weeks went by and the mayor grew impatient to see the work, restless to see himself set on high and although he knew he should not, the impatient magistrate went to spy on the masterpiece. 'Good master painter,' said he, 'I pray you let me see your work.' But Howleglas knew this moment would come. He may not have been a great artist, nor a creator of great works, but he was most certainly artful and a creator of goodly lies. 'Gladly, sir,' he replied, 'but first know this. Only those born in wedlock can see my work, which is a marvellous thing, for not only will you have a beautiful ceiling, but you will also know all those who are of dishonest birth in your company!' The mayor thought it was indeed a glorious conceit, for not only would he see himself raised up on high, but also he would see others of his acquaintance fall from grace. Fool that he was, the mayor knew well enough that knowledge was power, with power came prestige and perhaps even more portraits besides!

He followed Howleglas into the hall and up the scaffold where the mock artist pulled back the cloths and pointed to the false fresco that never was. 'Behold,' said Howleglas, 'there you sit in heaven above.' and he pointed to patches of bare rendered brick, on which he claimed the mayor's red robes flowed lightly over soft clouds and to another place where the sun glinted off Dame Fame's trumpet as she proclaimed his worthiness to rule over all. Howleglas described the pretend scene in detail, down to a point where the vaulted ceiling met the wall and where Howleglas said that he had painted the meaner sort peering up towards the mayor seated in the sky above, while one and all sang his praises. Well, the mayor could not see the painting, only the foul stains of age and neglect and the rough rendered walls, but he did not want to be known as a bastard, base-born out of wedlock, and so he praised the work, the fair colours and fine rendering of light. 'Your work pleases me greatly,' said the mayor, 'so fine is it that I wish others to see it.'

He fetched his wife so that she might see his grandeur and he might see something of her history besides. She came into the hall and climbed the scaffold as Howleglas told her of the strange properties of his painting, that only those born of married parents might gaze upon its beauty. Then he pulled back the sheet and showed her the mayor's red robes flowing lightly over soft clouds, the sun glinting off Dame Fame's trumpet as she proclaimed her husband's worthiness to rule over all and the place where the vaulted ceiling met the wall, where the meaner sort peered up towards the mayor seated in the firmament, one and all singing his praises. Well, the mayor's wife could not see the painting, only the foul stains of age and neglect and the rough rendered walls, but she did not want to be known as a bastard, base-born out of wedlock and so she went to her husband and praised the work, the fair colours and fine rendering of light. 'The work please me greatly,' said she, 'it is so fine I wish that others could see it.'

And so it went on as the mayor's most trusted servants were sent to gaze upon the work, while Howleglas told all in their turn of the fresco's wondrous properties and pointed to the mayor's red robes flowing lightly over soft clouds, the sun glinting off

Dame Fame's trumpet as she proclaimed their master's worthiness to rule over all and to the place where the vaulted ceiling met the wall, where the meaner sort looked up towards the mayor seated in the firmament, one and all singing his praises. And each in turn saw naught but the foul stains of age and neglect and the rough rendered walls, yet praised the painting as the finest fresco that they had ever seen.

The mayor tested each in turn and all proved worthy, but now he wished to show his greatness to a larger audience of aldermen, sheriffs and rich merchants of the city and county in which he lived. He ordered Howleglas to finish the fresco and to take his leave, collecting his payment as he went, for there was no place for an artisan such as he among the great company invited to the feast that the vain man had in mind. Howleglas, the beguiler of the foolish, the coney-catching cunning man was happy to go, for meetings of powerful men were of little interest to him and just a bit dangerous besides. He left quickly, taking his friends with him and gladly sharing the profits of his deceit.

As for the mayor? Well, he held a sumptuous banquet and invited the great and the good of his locality, so that they might gaze upon his greatness as he hoped to gaze upon their fall. But Howleglas was gone and so there was no one to tell them of the painting's strange and wondrous properties, nor point out the mayor's red robes flowing lightly over soft clouds, the sun glinting off Dame Fame's trumpet as she proclaimed his worthiness to rule over all, nor the place where the vaulted ceiling met the wall and where the meaner sort looked up towards the mayor seated in the firmament, one and all singing his praises.

And so it was that when the sheets were pulled down that evening the guests saw only the foul stains of age and neglect and the rough rendered walls, that spoke more of the mayor's character than a fair fresco ever could. They all laughed loudly at the great man's even greater foolishness, although none laughed so loud as the painter of false frescoes and his companions in cozenage, who were already far, far away. They all laughed loudly as Dame Fame blew upon her trumpet – a great blast upon the horn in honour of a certain trickster, a beguiler of the foolish, a coney-catching cunning man called Howleglas and that is why some of his stories grace the pages of this book!

Of Howleglas and the Village Without Sin

In 1564 William Bendthorpe was set in the stocks by Norwich marketplace for 'counterfeiting himself to be dumb and deceiving the Queen's liege people'. He was what was called a 'counterfeit crank', or a 'dummerer', men and women who feigned some illness or disability in order to exploit the charity of others.

Some counterfeit cranks were said to chew soap so that they appeared to be frothing at the mouth, while others rolled in nettles so that they looked as if they were suffering from some terrible disease of the flesh. The Tudor priest and commentator William Harrison stated that some poor beggars went even further and in his *Description of England* (1587) Harrison described how some 'idle people' applied corrosives 'to the fleshy parts of their bodies', using ratsbane, crowsfoot and spearwort to 'raise pitiful and odious sores'.[23] This evidence should be treated with caution for Harrison was contemptuous of many within the lower orders. I don't think such extreme cases were that common and for me they demonstrate the desperation of the poor in Elizabethan England.

It must be remembered that the late 1500s saw a change in attitudes towards the poor and beggars in particular. The Reformation saw a decline in charity and during the Elizabethan period there was the introduction of poor rates that angered many who were forced to pay them. Where once the well-meaning had been happy to give alms to the poor, many now felt that it was the duty of the overseers of poor relief. But the new centralised system was harsh and caused misery for many, something dealt with in greater detail elsewhere in this book. Suffice it to say the new poor laws went a long way to criminalising the poor and saw a rise in prosecutions of counterfeit cranks, as well as genuine beggars. The middling sort went to church to save their own souls, but were less happy saving their poorer neighbours. But perhaps such hypocrisy is natural and existed in earlier times as well, maybe even before the Tudor Reformation, when some only gave charity to ensure their own salvation and to demonstrate their piety. It's a preoccupation that Howleglas uses to his advantage in this tale of deceit …

✿ ✿ ✿

There was once a trickster, a beguiler of the foolish, a coney-catching cunning man called Howleglas who travelled from town to town, village to village and house to house wearing many different disguises. Sometimes a priest, sometimes a potter, sometimes a pedlar of wares, but on this day he arrived in a village disguised as a monk, a man of God, about his business cleansing the souls of the wicked. For Howleglas had heard tell that people of this place desired luxury and lechery most of all and loved gorging more than God. It was said that even the local priest cared more about dicing than the divine!

As Howleglas passed the churchyard he could see it was true, for there were holes in the thatch of the church roof and many of its windows were broken. And so it was, he waited until it was dark and with spade and lantern he set to work digging at the grave of a blacksmith long dead. He dug and he dug and he dug some more until at last spade struck bone and Howleglas had himself the skull of the blacksmith. It was a fine strong skull with jutting jaw and bold brow ridges and Howleglas cleaned and polished it to a shine. He had plans for this skull, for it was to rise above its station. 'From now on,' he thought, 'it is no longer the skull of a simple labouring man, instead it shall become the skull of St Brendan, the holiest of holy saints.' Howleglas the deceiver tucked his so recently acquired relic beneath his gown and went about his conning ways.

He went to the house of the priest, showed him the skull of St Brendan, and told him that the deceased man was 'the holiest of holy saints'. The priest was a simple soul and allowed Howleglas to preach on Sunday next and show the congregation the relic of St Brendan. He agreed that Howleglas would offer the skull up to all so that they might pay to touch it, for Howleglas's tongue was as cunning and quick as ever it had been, although his promise to split the profits with the priest may have also sweetened the uncomplicated cleric.

The following Sunday the church was packed as all had heard tell of the skull of St Brendan and all agreed that he was 'the holiest of holy saints'. Howleglas the mock monk climbed up into the pulpit and began to preach to all. He talked of God in heaven and the Devil in hell. He talked of Noah's deluge and of how an unfortunate fellow called Daniel fell into the lion's den. And when at last his knowledge of all things religious was spent, the king of cozenage pulled the skull of the blacksmith from beneath his robes, holding the relic high for all to see. 'Behold,' he called, 'this is the skull of St Brendan, holiest of holy saints. And I have brought him to your village this day to save your souls!' Howleglas banged his fist upon the pulpit and gestured in dramatic fashion as he continued preaching to the disconcerted. 'For so pure was St Brendan in life,' said he, 'that those who kiss his skull, they too shall be cleansed. Their ills shall be cured and they shall be guaranteed their place in heaven above.' And now the mock monk stared hard at the crowd. 'But!' said Howleglas to the wide-eyed congregation, 'So pure was St Brendan in life that only the pure can touch his skull, it cannot be sullied by sin. Only those among you who have not committed foul deeds may pay what you can to kiss his skull.' Now pointing at one and all, for the mock monk knew all the tricks of his trickster trade, Howleglas said, 'Any here who have sinned, all who are drunkards, cuckolds, thieves or worse, they must remain in their seats, for I shall not receive the sullied coin of rogues, knaves or whoremongers this day!' And now Howleglas held out the skull for the congregation to kiss, while the priest rung a bell loudly and began to chant.

Well, it may have only been the skull of a blacksmith taken a few nights' since from its grave, but now men and women, old and young, rich and poor came forward, all pushing and jostling so that they might pay to kiss the counterfeit relic. They offered all they had from a few poor pennies to gold, silver and jewels to prove to all that they were not sinners, while those who had sinned most were first in the queue, giving the rings off their fingers to prove to everyone else that they had not sinned at all! Howleglas accepted all coin from all comers, touching their heads and uttering sham Latin benedictions to all. He assured each and every member of the congregation that they were without sin and would be saved that day, while Howleglas, be he saint or sinner, saved or no, was certainly very rich. And watching him leave the village without sin, weighed down with all their coin, I think that it is fair to say that he was guaranteed a good life in this world, if not the next!

OF HOWLEGLAS AND THE MIRACLE CURE

ricksters like Howleglas played upon the fears of others and in the story below it was the fear of the plague, a disease that was rampant in Tudor England. An outbreak in 1579 killed an estimated 5,000 people in Norwich alone.[24]

No one knew how to stop it, but that's not to say they did not try. Boatmen were ordered to 'air' letters brought from other places and chains were hung across rivers to prevent unauthorised ships mooring at city quays. Players and performers were banned from entering cities and people suspected of having the plague were sealed in their houses in an attempt to stop the spread of infection. The watch was posted outside houses to supply food and water to those sealed in and also to prevent victims escaping; not that it always worked. Phineous Gibson escaped from a nailed-up house and so he was sent to the 'pest house', a temporary prison set up during times of plague. The one in Norwich was in a tower of the old medieval city walls. During his incarceration in the tower pest house Gibson was at least compensated three shillings weekly, to help pay for food and other comforts. These were tense times, so the authorities had to be seen to be fair.

Gibson was not alone, for both the men who buried the dead and the women employed to search the dead, to see who had or had not died of plague, were also forced to stay in the towers when their work was done. Men were also employed killing dogs, cats, pigs and any other animals left loose on the streets, while merchants and other businessmen were ordered to take down the awnings outside their shops, because it was feared that they trapped the foul odours that some believed caused the plague.

Not that everyone agreed with this, as in the late summer of 1602 when the Mayor of Norwich, Thomas Lane, was walking the streets of the city checking that all were keeping to the regulations for the control of the plague and other diseases. When he arrived at the property of the beer brewer and alderman Robert Gybson, the mayor saw that he had not taken the awnings down in front of his shop. He ordered Gybson to remove the said awnings, but he would not and the two fell to arguing:

> Mr Gybson in spiteful and scornful manners said, 'I would see who dare pull them down', to which Mr Mayor answered, 'that dare I', and did take hold of one of the hangings and pulled it down, whereupon Mr Gybson, in the hearing of a great number of people, used many reproachful, scornful, contemptuous, and foul speeches and unfitting behaviour, and to disgrace him what he could … [and] shortly after a libel was cast abroad containing much matter of distain and slander against the Mr Mayor, his children and family.

So serious was the libel against Mayor Lane that Robert Gybson was stripped of the office of alderman and freeman and was 'to be treated henceforth as a foreigner'.

These were difficult times that prevented people from going about their daily business. Times were hard and many like Gybson felt it necessary to ignore the plague orders. Men like William Patrick, a boatman who was placed in stocks because he did 'bring Lydel's wife from Yarmouth in his boat even though a Scotsman had died of infection in her house'. Perhaps more desperate still was John Hastings who was also put in stocks for 'robbing the clothes of the deceased of the plague and the selling thereof'. Here was a man willing to risk catching the plague to earn some coin and it was desperation such as this that helped con men and tricksters like Howleglas …

There was once a trickster, a beguiler of the foolish, a coney-catching cunning man called Howleglas who travelled from town to town, village to village and house to house wearing many different disguises. Sometimes a priest, sometimes a potter, sometimes a pedlar of wares, but on this day he arrived in a certain town disguised as a doctor of physic. He went abroad claiming that he could cure any ill. Whether you had the sweating sickness, the pestilence, or the pox, Dr Howleglas would cure it, for a price of course!

Well, it just so happened that the director of a local hospital had many patients in his care whom he could not cure and having heard of Howleglas's great skill at medicine, he paid the false doctor a visit at the inn where he now stayed. And Howleglas said, 'Why yes, I can cure any ill. Whether your patients have the sweating sickness, the pestilence, or the pox, I shall cure it, for a price of course!' And so it was the two men agreed a contract – that the director should pay Howleglas one hundred pounds if he could cure all the poorly patients. But so confident was our counterfeit quack that he said that he would not take one penny if but one of the patients was not healed.

The director was a man who knew the value of money and valued the 'chinks' above all other things. One hundred pounds was a lot of money, ten years' wages for a labouring man, but not paying a penny for the medic's ministrations was worth the risk. The two shook hands and agreed that Howleglas should attend the hospital the following day. The very next morning he arrived at the hospital early and was given a small chamber in which he might examine the patients one by one by one.

One by one by one the ailing men and women were brought before the cunning leech. One by one by one they told him their tales of woe. Of the boils on their backs, of the boils on their bellies and the boils on every part of their bodies, for let's just say that some of them had not sat comfortably for the longest of times! Howleglas nodded knowingly as each patient in turn listed their ailments. The deceitful doctor tut, tut, tutted in all the right places, while he scribbled and scraped, scraped and scribbled with quill pen upon parchment. And when at last each in turn had finished telling all there was to tell of their many afflictions, Howleglas drew them in close and said: 'Listen, friend, I like you. I like your face and so I have a secret to tell you, a secret that you must promise to tell no other. Do you swear?' And only when each patient in turn had sworn upon their very soul not to tell another living soul, did Howleglas continue beguiling each in turn. 'Good,' whispered he, 'then know this. If I am to cure you all then I must first find the sickest one among you to burn, so that I can use their ashes to make a medicine that the rest of you will drink. If I am to cure you all,' said Howleglas triumphantly, 'I must find the sickest one among you to burn!'

Having told each of the patients the very same story Dr Howleglas went into the hall of the hospital where he ordered the servants to set and light a great fire. He asked that all the patients be carried into the hall and now the trickster stood upon a bench so that all could see, while he called out, 'Let he or she who is the sickest one here step forward.' But none stepped forward and so it was the cunning con man went from one to the next, asking one after the other, 'Are you the sickest one here?' But all said, 'No'. They said that they were 'not sick at all'. They all claimed that they were 'cured', and that it was 'a miracle cure!' And even though some of the patients at the hospital had scarce walked in many a year, all now ran quickly from that place.

The fictitious physician's work was done. The patients were cured for a day or two at least. The director of the hospital was happy for a day or two at least and as for Dr Howleglas? Well, he was very rich and more than a little merry for a long, long time to come!

OF JUDGEMENTS WELL MADE

n 1606 Peter Pynfold was whipped for 'coney catch-ing and drunkenness'. It may have been a new century and a new dynasty on the throne of England, but Pynfold had appeared before the court many times, in both the late 1500s and early 1600s. Perhaps his drunkenness stemmed from his success and subsequent celebrations at conning others, although it is just as likely that it was the result of luring the gul-lible into alehouses where men like him often plied their trade. For what better way to con a coney than to get him drunk first?

That's exactly what happened to John Denman and his is an interesting case, because thus far the stories and records in this section have focused on tricksters, the men and women who made their living cheating others. But what of their victims, what happened to them? In truth, we know very little, although as with the case of Denman we do have the odd insight into their woes. John appeared before the Norwich mayor's court in 1551 and made complaint that he had been cheated at numerous games of dice in the Angel Inn in the city. In total he claimed to have lost five pairs of gloves, a silver whistle, a dagger, fifty-five shillings, thirty-five of which he borrowed from an opponent, and a shirt worth twelve shillings! What happened to Denman I do not know, but when it comes to other victims of the trickster's art, well in stories at least they might find some sympathy and wisdom on the part of those judging their cases …

As with many of my tales this one starts with a poor man, for there were many paupers long ago, some of whom made their living by begging, some by labouring and others by robbing from honest folk. But the poor man in this story was an honest man who got by as best he could. Life was hard until the day he found a great purse full of coin, which he took home to his wife. They counted the coin and found there to be a thousand crowns in total and both began to dream of how best to spend it, to make their hard lives a little more tolerable than ever they had been before.

But the rich man, the merchant who had lost it, was not so ready to let the money go. He paid the bellmen of the city to make cry and call out that whosoever returned the missing purse would be rewarded with one hundred of the crowns within. The poor man heard the calls and went to his wife, telling her that they must return the purse to the rich man. His wife agreed, saying that 'a hundred crowns earned by honest means, would see greater riches in heaven than a thousand gained by deception'.

And so it was, the poor man returned the coin to the rich man, although the merchant was not as honest as the poor man's wife, nor so devout. He was as skilled in falsehood as ever he was at buying and selling and now he claimed that the poor man had not given back all the coin that was in his purse, that there had been fourteen hundred crowns when it was lost. 'When you give me my other four hundred crowns,' said the merchant, 'then I shall give you your one hundred crowns reward.'

The poor man lacked wealth but not pride, and he took his case to the mayor of his town who listened to the poor man's plea, although he knew not what to do. Setting the price of corn and keeping the streets clear of butchers' offal were the limits of his ability and so he passed the case to a judge who had come recently to that place to ply his trade. He was said to be a wise man in all things and so the mayor asked for his help. The judge listened to both the rich man's and the poor man's arguments, tut, tut, tutting in all the right places, nodding only where necessary and scribbling and scraping with pen upon parchment when such facts as were important to the case were given.

The learned judge asked the poor man: 'Didst thou truly find a purse with one thousand crowns within?' 'Yes,' the poor man replied. He asked the rich man: 'Didst thou truly lose a purse with fourteen hundred crowns within?' 'Yes,' the rich man replied. The judge, having heard both men's side in the case, went away and pondered upon his judgement and as I'm sure many of you know that's the best kind of thinking there is, well suited to a serious case such as this!

At the next sitting of the court he made plain his judgement saying that both the rich and the poor man were clearly honest fellows, the first having grown rich through honest trading and the second having remained poor through honestly returning that which was not his. And so as both were honest men then the purse containing the thousand crowns could not be the purse of the rich man and since no other had laid claim to it, then the poor man may keep it for himself. 'And,' proclaimed the judge, 'when the other purse containing fourteen hundred crowns is found, then it shall be returned to the merchant!'

Well, the rich merchant saw that the wise judge had seen through his false ways and that he had stumbled into a ditch of his own digging. Seeing no way out, the rich man pleaded for lenience. Mercy was granted, although the poor man was still given his hundred crowns reward and the merchant was from that day forward known to be a man of ill fame and evil behaviour. A man whose fraudulent ways left him poorer in more ways than one!

The wise judge, he too enjoyed the rewards that good judgements bring, for the mayor asked him to stay in his city a while longer and adjudicate in other cases where cozenage was suspected. And so it was that he heard tell of a poor farmer who had had many a goose stolen by Swaine's wife, yet he could not prove her guilty of the crime. The two were brought before the judge to argue their cases and he listened to both the poor farmer and Swaine's wife carefully. He tut, tut, tutted in all the right places, nodding only where necessary and scribbling and scraping with pen upon parchment when such facts as were important to the case were given. Once again he pondered the case thoroughly, but still he was unable to decide between them.

He was not beaten though, for now the clever judge sent out warrants ordering that the poor farmer, Swaine's wife and many others of the town who had done naught wrong were to appear before the next session of the court. All were summoned into the judgement chamber where the learned judge, the mayor and his aldermen looked on. All took their ease upon long benches set out in rows in front of the judge's bench, while he stood up and spoke to all resting there. 'Why do you not sit down?' asked the judge, while all gathered before him looked bemused. 'Why, sir,' they all replied, 'we sit down already.' But the judge shook his head, 'Oh no you do not,' he said, 'for the one who stole the poor man's geese is standing up still, she sitteth not!' Leaping to her feet, Swaine's wife cried 'Oh yes I do!' Although now of course the guilty woman was on her feet and when at last she did sit again it was in the stocks. There she sat with a plucked goose about her neck, a reminder of her crimes!

Not long after, a soldier was brought before the judge; a man whose deeds were so foul that he should have been hanged. But whether it was the fact the man was a soldier who had served his masters well in times of war, or perhaps it was that the judge saw in the man a wit equal to his own, I do not know. Whatever the cause he allowed the guilty fellow to grasp at redemption. 'By rights you should die for your terrible crimes,' said the judge, 'but if you can tell the court three unshakeable truths this day, I shall let you walk free.' The soldier had nothing to lose but all to gain, and so for his first truth he spoke thus: 'Since I was a youth I have been of bad character.' The judge and his court could not argue with the solider and accepted his words and so asked the guilty man to continue. He did and for the second truth he spoke thus: 'I fear for my life this day.' Again none in the court could argue with the soldier, for none would have willingly taken his place! And so it was, the soldier proceeded with his wise words and for the third truth he spoke thus: 'If I am allowed to walk free of this place, I will never willingly come back here.' The court scratched their heads over his statement, but not the judge. 'You have answered truthfully,' said he, 'so go now and never come back!'

Well, the gifted judge had again proven himself wise beyond measure, but who he really was, no one knew. I like to think that he was a certain cozener and beguiler of men, a con man about his tricks, wearing yet another different disguise. For there is another short tale that I wish to relate in which three men go to an alehouse, perhaps the two poor men and the judge from the stories above – the pauper who found the purse and the other who lost his goose, but not the wise villain who had just walked free from the court, for he had vowed to stay away from such places that can easily bring a good man low! Perhaps the two poor men wished to buy the judge some meat and ale by way of a thank you for his shrewd services, for the clever and cunning judgements he made on their behalves.

But the judge's cunning had yet to be used up this day, for as the three men ate and drank their fill, they admired their hostess, the alewife who ran the tavern in which they now sat. She was a fair creature and it was clear to all that she was seeking company this night. All three men fell to arguing about who should attend her, even the poor man who was already wed.

They were close to scrapping, when the wisest one among them suggested that they divide her into three parts.

The other two agreed, one of the poor men saying, 'If this fair women is to be shared among us, then I shall want her head and face so that we can kiss whenever I wish.' The second poor fellow said, 'Then I shall have her breast, for there beats her heart, the organ of love and it shall be forever mine.' The third and wisest of the three and the one who had suggested her division in the first place, he said, 'Then I am left with her buttocks and below and I shall have to be content.'

Their choices well made, the three men ate and drank their fill and then made ready to depart the alewife's inn, but as they left the third man grabbed the hostess and kissed her long and deep. The first who had lain claim to her lips chided the third, 'How could you,' he cried, 'how could you kiss that which is mine?' But the third simply smiled at the first and bid him not be so angry, for as he said, 'I give you permission to kiss my part of the alewife in return!'

And so the three departed no longer friends, but the wisest one had the last laugh and a long deep kiss, a goodly memory to fuel his dreams for many nights to come. Perhaps he carried that memory in a sack full of diverse disguises, including a doctor's cap, an unused paintbrush and a blacksmith's skull. And if you who are reading this story feel as bemused as the innocent folk who sat in the mayor's court long ago, if you do not understand why it pleases me so, then you have yet to read the tales of Howleglas also set down in this book for your enjoyment.

CHAPTER VI

THE MANY-HEADED MONSTER

OF THE YEOMAN'S WIFE

Beat all Beggars

hen Tudor merchant John Southill died in1498 he left 'six quarters of rye to the poorest people in these six parishes'. Bequests like this were not uncommon, not least because in pre-Reformation England, it was believed that good works helped speed a benefactor's soul through purgatory and hopefully on into heaven. But things were about to change and although bequests continued, the Reformation in England saw a growing apathy towards the poor.

The change in attitude was subtle, but progressive; thus when Henry Keeble, a London grocer, died in 1511, he left one hundred marks to pay for poor women's dowries and to buy ploughshares and other tools for poor husbandmen. But, when Sir Thomas Roe, a London merchant, died in 1568, he merely lent one hundred pounds to eight poor men.[25] Both men left bequests to help the poor and to get them back to work, but Roe's bequest, I think, reflects the growing view that there were two types of poor: the 'deserving', the old and sick; and the 'undeserving', often referred to as 'sturdy beggars'. The distinction is summed up well by Robert Crawley in a poem of 1550:

The beggars whom need compelleth to crave,
Ought at our hands some relief to have,
But such as do counterfeit having their strength
To labour if they lust, being known at the length.
Ought to be constrained to work as they can,
And live on their labours, as be seemeth a Christian. [26]

From 1571 the Norwich orders for the poor provided grain stores and education for poor boys, but this was a 'carrot and stick' system, a punitive system of control, for as the order stated, from then on, "no person should need to go a begging nor be suffered to beg within the said city".[27] The Elizabethan poor laws may have started in Norwich, but they were soon rolled out across the country and everywhere begging was banned without a licence, while anyone caught harbouring a beggar could be fined, whipped or even lose an ear.

The cost of living rose by 40 per cent between 1584 and 1600 in England, but wages remained low. Enclosure forced many poorer people off the land and frequent poor harvests, especially in the 1590s, caused great hardship and need. There was a growing gap between rich and poor and many from the middling sort thrived under the tough economic conditions. Yeoman farmers bought up the smaller farms of those who had been forced off the land. And engrossing like this brought great rewards. In the 1560s a servant of husbandry earned about twenty-six shillings and eight pence per year, yet a yeoman farmer could expect to make between three hundred and five hundred pounds. Others, of course, made even more. Sir Henry Percy's household accounts for 1585–87 show that he spent thirty-eight pounds and four shillings just on 'diverse hawks' used for hunting, while Norfolk gentleman Nathaniel Bacon spent over two hundred pounds on one dress and jewels for his daughter's wedding.[28]

The rise in poverty saw a continual rise in the poor rates used to fund the new poor laws and growing anger and resentment on the part of those who had to pay them. However, this was matched by the anger and frustration on the part of the poor who were crowded into slum housing and forced into back-breaking work to survive, all of which helps explain stories like this one …

There was a very common saying long ago that 'the LOVE of money is the root of all evil'. Another stated that 'it is more blessed to GIVE than to receive'. These were commonly held beliefs among the pious and well-meaning people of long ago, but not all heeded such good advice. Not all in Tudor times were willing to share their wealth.

For there was once a yeoman's wife whose husband was a farmer, a man of property who had increased the size of his farm yearly, by buying up the land of his struggling neighbours and fencing it off to raise sheep. For as any a Tudor man of business could have told you, there was money to be made in wool! Sheep now grazed where once poor men had eked out a living, growing crops and taking what they needed from the land. But when sheep came, the poorer farmers were forced to go and the very same opportunities that saw the yeoman farmer grow fat and rich transformed his neighbours into vagrants and vagabonds, begging and stealing a crust wheresoever they could.

But the farmer died. He was taken by the plague and all that had been his was now his wife's and she lived well off the profits of her farm. While most of her neighbours lay upon straw, she slept on a soft feather mattress. A soft feather mattress that sat on a carved oak bed so much more comfortable than the hard earth floor where most of her neighbour's straw palliasses were laid. A carved oak bed set within a chamber bedecked with painted hangings and cushions, the like of which her neighbours would never know, for few were allowed into the yeoman's wife's house, unless it was to cook and clean for her. That's not to say that she did not have guests. She did, for there were many of the better sort the woman wished to impress with her hospitality and her fine pewter plates displayed upon a cupboard for all to see. She liked others to see the rewards of hard work, although in truth she did very little of that hard work herself! Instead she had servants to do her bidding – to light her fires, milk her cows, churn her milk into butter and to feed her pigs with whatever scraps were left upon the dinner table. The yeoman's wife told others what to do and watched closely how they did it. Especially when it came to the care of her swine. The yeoman's wife was very fond of her six pigs, for soon she would sell them at market and make a handsome profit.

She loved money and swine most of all and in that order, but not even coin can buy eternal life. The plague came again and now it was time for the yeoman's wife to go. She lay stricken by the pestilence that preyed upon rich and poor alike. Her soft feather mattress was no longer a comfort to her and she lay upon her bed with her friends and family gathered about her, making her last will and testament. Some listened intently, hoping for a share of the yeoman's wife's wealth, while others wept bitter tears, wishing that she would at last make her peace with God, hoping that she might make some charitable bequests and so prepare her soul for heaven. Her daughter, who loved her more than she deserved, leant close by her dying mother and said that she should leave grain from her barn to the poor of the parish. But her mother shook her head and said, 'NO!' For the yeoman's wife had no time for the poor. She complained that she was taxed too much already to support the old, the sick and impoverished who were unable to care for themselves. She complained that there were far too many masterless vagrants wandering the roads causing trouble wherever they went. 'They are nothing but sturdy beggars,' she said, 'lazy idle loiterers and bed-pressers. Rogues, even, who would cut your throat as soon as look at you.' The yeoman's wife thought them all vagabonds who should be whipped out of her village to go back from whence they came. 'And if they should return,' said the yeoman's wife, 'they should be hanged.' And she meant it, for such was her dislike of the poor and the sick that she would not even give them the scraps off her table. Instead, the yeoman's wife fed them to her pigs, for as she was so often fond of saying, 'I would rather be a pig than a beggar!'

The dying woman's family feared that their mother would not find rest unless she changed her ways. And so it was the yeoman's wife's son who loved his mother less than his sister did, but still more than the old woman deserved, leant close by his dying mother and said that she should leave money to the poor, so that they might buy tools and so find work wherever it might be found. But the old woman shook her head and said, 'NO!' For the yeoman's wife had no time for the poor. She complained that they wasted what little money they had playing at dice and cards in the alehouse and tavern, while watching cock kill cock and dog savage bear. 'They are nothing but knaves and churls,' she said, 'who would cut your purse and get drunk on their ill-gotten gains.' The yeoman's wife thought them all vagabonds who should be whipped out of her village to go back from whence they came. 'And if they should return,' said the yeoman's wife, 'they should be hanged.' And she meant it, for such was her dislike of the poor and the sick that she would not even give them the scraps off her table. Instead, the yeoman's wife fed them to her pigs, for as she was so often fond of saying, 'I would rather be a pig than a beggar!'

Most who heard the old woman's words took little notice, some even believing she spoke the truth. Yet those closest to the dying woman wished to see her at peace. Her parish priest, who loved the old woman's soul if not the old woman herself, leant in close and said that she should leave coin to the sick in the hospital or those festering in gaol, unable to pay fines and so buy their way out. But the yeoman's wife shook her head and said, 'NO!' For the yeoman's wife had no time for the poor, sick or prisoners. She complained that they were nothing but filthy, diseased vagrants. 'I have often heard tell,' said she, 'that cunning beggars put ratsbane, crowfoot and other poisons upon their bodies to raise pitiful sores, so that they might play upon the foolish pity of well folk like you.' The yeoman's wife thought them all con men and tricksters who should be whipped out of her village to go back from whence they came. 'And if they should return,' said the yeoman's wife, 'they should be hanged.' And she meant it, for such was her dislike of the poor and the sick that she would not even give them the scraps off her table. Instead, the yeoman's wife fed it to her pigs, for as she was so often fond of saying, 'I would rather be a pig than a beggar!'

The old woman's family feared that the doors of heaven would be firmly barred to her, for now it was too late. The yeoman's wife was dead. But life goes on and the following day the old woman's servants rose early as they always did and went about their business: they lit the fires, milked the cows and churned the milk into butter. One of the servants went to feed the dead woman's pigs with whatever scraps were left over from the dinner table. But as she poured the scraps into the trough she screamed loudly, dropped the bucket and ran back to the house, for where there had once been six pigs, now there were seven slurping greedily from the trough. Where that seventh pig came from I will let you decide. Suffice it to say that it was much bigger and fatter than the rest and as it nipped at the other swine and gorged itself upon leftover scraps, it was easy to see that it felt some natural right to take all that it wanted. Even if it meant that there was less for the rest!

OF THE MAN WHO PAID WITH NAUGHT

n 1597, *An Act For Punnishment of Rogues, Vagabonds and Sturdy Beggars* dictated that

All jugglers, tinkers, pedlars and petty chapmen wandering abroad, all wandering persons and common labourers being persons able of body using loitering and refusing to work for such reasonable wages [and] all persons delivered out of gaols that beg for their fees [and] all such persons that shall wander abroad begging pretending losses by fire or otherwise: and all such persons not being felons wandering and pretending themselves to be Egyptians, or wandering in the habit form or attire of counterfeit Egyptians: shall be taken adjudged and deemed Rogues, Vagabonds and Sturdy Beggars, and shall sustain such pain and punishment as by this Act is in that behalf appointed.[29]

It's evidence of the growing fear of 'the many-headed monster' in late Tudor England. A common enough term for vagrants at the time, it referred to the growing body of poor men, women and children who were forced off the land by enclosure, to wander the roads in search of work, while begging for food and coin. Many complained of how the enclosure of common land was leading to the 'decay of England',[30] but it fell on deaf ears, the authorities punishing the vagrants instead. Such was the concern that Elizabethan statutes made it legal for vagrants to be whipped out of a town or city for a first offence, and to have a hole burnt in their ear, or even to be hanged, should they keep coming back.

The anxiety that this group generated was not helped by the fact that many vagrants travelled in groups for their own protection, but this only added to the fear that they were gangs who would cut your throat as soon as look at you. Much of this was propaganda on the part of the Tudor state, although some vagrants were dangerous. Men like Thomas Draper of Nottinghamshire, who was whipped out of Norwich for being found 'wandering in the city and for that he seemeth a dangerous rogue, for that hath been branded on his shoulder'. Richard Griffin was whipped about the market for being a vagrant and for 'very evil behaviour'.

There was also concern over a group that modern academics refer to as 'itinerant polygamists'. A new phenomenon in Tudor England that grew out of the Reformation and subsequent rise in radical Protestant sects such as the Anabaptists, Familists and Antinomians; groups that challenged established ideas and beliefs and even traditional moral values. They included couples like Edward Ainsworth and Margery King, who were both whipped out of Norwich for leading 'a lewd life and that they lived together as man and wife, but they were never married'. William Dryver and Anne Hamersley 'were found in the town as vagrants and upon examination found and confessed that they travelled about the country as man and wife where indeed they were never married, but have lived disorderly therefore it is ordered that they shall be thoroughly whipped at the post'.

Beggars, vagabonds and radical Protestants who stole for a living and rejected church teachings were a source of tension and conflict. The legislation against them grew particularly harsh in late Tudor England and there was many a story that warned of the dangers of the stranger upon the road …

There was once a man who was very poor. He made what little coin he had doing work that was guided by the seasons. In summer he would cart other people's goods from here to there and even somewhere else for that matter. During the cold, bleak winter months he would dig ditches, but the work was hard and the poor man had little to look forward to in life. And so it was he was a man whose head was turned very easily, a man who like many of us today always wanted more. He always wanted that which he could not have.

For one day when he was walking home along the road the poor man met a pedlar coming the other way, a pedlar carrying a pack upon his back and calling out, 'What do you lack, what do you lack, what will you buy from the pack on my back?' The pedlar was selling all manner of wares from the wicker basket hanging from his shoulders, from pots to potions to pins and everything in between. But on this particular day, this particular pedlar was also selling a fine, fine knife and the poor man gazed longingly upon it. Sunlight danced up and down the blade, a blade that looked sharp enough to draw blood from the very wind that whistled about the poor man's cold bare legs. Then there was the hilt, the handle of the dagger – a gold thread ran up and around that hilt till it met a great jewel at the top. Now what sort of jewel it was the poor man did not know, for he was a simple man much like me, but he felt certain that such a stone was fine enough to grace a king's crown. He felt certain that if he could have that dagger hanging from his belt, then it would show him to be a man of great worth. Someone of great importance! Oh how he wished the knife could be his.

Alas, though, as the pedlar told the poor man it was indeed a fine blade, a knife worthy of a knight or nobleman no less, a dagger worth forty shillings or more, which was a fortune to a poor man such as he. With such an amount a man could buy many fine things, from a hogshead of sack wine to a silver goblet to serve it in. The poor man had no choice but to walk away, but as he did, the pedlar called him back. 'Hold on, hold on,' said he, 'for we haven't finished talking yet, you and I. For I can see that you like this 'ere knife and do you know what? The knife likes you. I can see that if you had this knife hanging from your the belt it would show you to be a man of great worth. Someone of great importance!' And now the pedlar suggested that he and the poor man do a deal – that he give the knife to the poor man for free. 'You can have the dagger for nothing,' said the pedlar, 'as long as you pay me with something worth naught when I come a calling in seven days' time.'

Well, the poor man thought this was a good bargain and the two shook hands to seal the deal. But no sooner had they shaken hands that the pedlar spoke once more, 'Wait,' said he, 'wait, for if when I return in seven days' time you can't pay me with something worth nothing, then I shall have my forty shillings and if I can't have my forty shillings, then I shall want your soul!' The pedlar was not really a pedlar, for the pedlar was the Devil in disguise. Had the poor man looked down he would have seen the Devil's hairy legs, his cloven horny hooves sticking out from beneath the pedlar's coat, but he had not and now it was too late. The deal had been done, there was to be no going back and the poor man was forced to take the knife home with him. A fine blade it was, which had it been hanging from the poor man's belt then it would have shown him to be a man of great worth, someone of great importance. But now it was hidden in the poor man's pack, for he was more concerned with thinking of something worth naught with which he could pay the Devil himself!

Well, I think I know what many of you are thinking; that there is nothing worth naught in this world. Even the air we breathe has value, for without it we would surely die. Even a stone has value, for it can be used to build a house, or struck against iron to create a spark, a spark that can be used to make fire, a fire that can be fed by a twig, for even a simple stick has value and can be used to make the wattle walls of a poor man's hovel, a wattle wall that can be plastered with daub – simple mud walls, for even mud had value long ago. And so it was the poor man could think of nothing worth naught. And so it was he sat by the fire for seven days trying oh so hard to think of something with no value. He did not eat. He did not sleep. He did not work for seven days and because he had not earned any coin for a week or more his wife came into the room and demanded to know what was wrong. And because the poor man had not slept for seven days he fell to his knees sobbing before his wife as he confessed of the dagger and the Devil.

Alas though, no sooner had he fallen to his knees, no sooner had the poor man confessed of the dagger and the Devil, than there came a loud knock at the door … BANG, BANG, BANG. 'Oh no,' said the poor man, 'it's the Devil come to take me.'

Again he fell to his knees and as he did he saw a feather, a feather from a goose that his wife had just plucked. 'That's it,' cried the poor man, 'for surely a feather has no value. I shall give a feather to the Devil.' But think on; think of long, long ago. Could he really give a feather to the Devil, has a feather no value, for what can you do with feathers? Well, as I'm sure many of you know feathers had many uses in Tudor times; from the stuffing for a rich man's pillow to making a quill pen, from fletching an arrow to looking really, really good in a Tudor man's cap.

As the poor man's wife told him that there were many uses for a feather, there came another loud knock at the door … BANG, BANG, BANG. 'Oh no,' said the poor man, 'it's the Devil come to take me.' He fell to his knees as desperate men are wont to do and as he did he saw some straw, some straw he his wife had swept into the corner of the room. 'That's it,' cried the poor man, 'for surely straw has no value. I shall give straw to the Devil.' But think on; think of long, long ago. Could he really give straw to the Devil, has straw no value, for what can you do with straw? Well, as I'm sure some of you know, straw had many uses in the time of the Tudors; from the stuffing of a poor man's pillow to the weaving of a hat to keep the sun off a stout yeoman farmer's head, from providing tinder to light a fire, to mixing with mud for a fair and fine daub.

As the poor man's wife told him that there were many uses for straw there came another loud knock at the door … BANG, BANG, BANG. 'Oh no,' said the poor man, 'it's the Devil come to take me.' He threw himself into the corner of the room and turned his head to the wall. He was hoping if he could not see the Devil, then the Devil would not see him, but as did he sniffed the air, for now the poor man could smell dung. It was the muck of man and beast piled high on cart outside. 'That's it,' cried the poor man, 'for surely dung has no value. I shall give dung to the Devil.' Well, it sounds good doesn't it and after all, who wouldn't want to give dung to the Devil? But think on;

think of long, long ago. Could he really give dung to the Devil, has dung no value, for what can you do with dung? Well, as I'm sure a few of you know, dung had many uses some five hundred years ago; from patching a poor man's daub walls, to feeding the flowers in a rich man's knot garden, from drying out and burning on the fire, to throwing at the storytellers of long ago!

As the poor man's wife told him that there were many uses for dung there came a loud knock at the door ... BANG, BANG, BANG. 'Oh no,' said the poor man, 'it's the Devil come to take me.' He fell to his knees sobbing before his wife fearing that the Devil would finally take ownership of his soul. But his wife grew angry. Angry at the deal her husband had done. Angrier still that that she had the Devil himself beating loudly upon her door! She clipped her husband soundly about the ear. 'Off to town with you, foolish man,' said she, 'I shall deal with this well enough.' And no sooner had her husband left than the wife fetched a narrow-necked empty pot. It just happened to be her husband's pisspot, but we need say no more about that. She placed that pot high on a shelf so that none, not even the tallest, could see inside. Then and only then did she let the Devil in her door and before he had a chance to speak she said to him, 'I know your errand well enough, Old Hob. You've come for payment haven't you?' The Devil leered. 'Yes,' said he, 'yes I have.' 'Well,' said the woman, 'reach up into yonder pot and take what is rightfully yours.'

The Devil stood up high upon his horny hoofs, reached up into the pot and he began to feel around. And what do you think that he felt in there? I ask even though I'm sure many of you know. Nothing could be simpler than the answer to this riddle, for there was nothing in the pot! 'Well,' said the woman, 'you asked for nothing and now you have nothing. Be off with you, Devil, and bother us no more.' The Devil himself smashed the pot upon the floor, angry at having lost the man's soul. He was angrier still that he had been tricked by a woman! The Devil, however, never stays too angry for long, for he was content in the knowledge that he would meet many a less fortunate fool, many a less fortunate man on the road that very same day.

OF HE WHO SAID NE'ER A PENNY

In 1623, Dr Burman left monies to the poor of all the Norwich wards and also to prisoners held within the city 'for those held in the old castle, six shillings and eight pence, in the Guildhall, six shillings and eight pence and to those held in the Bridewell, two shillings and eight pence'. The good doctor's bequests were a demonstration of both his wealth and his godliness, a demonstration that he was one of the 'elect', who was worthy of going to heaven. But, a century earlier, before the Reformation and when England was still a Catholic country, such bequests were thought of as a prerequisite for salvation.

When for example William Worsley, the Dean of St Paul's in London, died in 1499 he left three pounds, six shillings and eight pence to be doled out to the poor on the day of his burial, in the hope and expectation that they would say prayers for the good of his soul. While in his will, Robert Jannys, merchant and former mayor of Norwich, wrote: 'I give my burying day to blind and sore within the city and at every gate about Norwich (hospitals in the old medieval gates) to the sisters of the Normans (another hospital) to every prisoner in the castle and guildhall, to every one of these four pence.' He also bequeathed 'that there be dealt on my burying day to every person that will take alms within their parish, one pence to pray for my soul'.[31] In pre-Reformation England, men and women left a lot of money to save their souls and many a poor person sought them out ...

There was once a trickster, a beguiler of the foolish, a coney-catching cunning man who may have been Howleglas, but then again not. For there were many con men on the road long ago, so you will appreciate that it was difficult for me to tell. Sometimes this particular trickster was a priest, sometimes a potter, sometimes a pedlar of wares, but on this day he arrived in a certain town disguised as a poor beggar.

For in a certain town and certainly long ago there was a rich man who lay dying with his family and few friends gathered close about him. All his life he had been a miser, the pursuit of wealth had been his religion, but now as his life grew less and less, his fear of the fires of hell grew more and more. And so it was, as he lay gasping his last upon his deathbed, he willed a penny to every poor beggar who said a prayer for his soul when he died. But so fearful was the miser that his money would be ill spent that he willed his coin should only go to honest men. 'For the good of my soul in heaven above,' he whispered, 'you must only give a penny to every poor beggar who speaks the truth. Those who tell lies, they shall have nothing.'

Having spoken these words, the rich miser died. Few mourned his passing, yet a great crowd of paupers and other needful folk gathered for his funeral. No sooner was he buried in the ground than his friends returned to the dead man's house so that they might dole out a penny to the virtuous poor.

The first beggar was shown in to stand before the executors of the miser's will and with head held low he mumbled, 'God is good.' The miser's friends were well pleased by his words. 'You speak the truth,' said the eldest and wisest among them, 'so you shall have a penny. Rejoice!' They sent him on his way with a penny and many blessings besides.

A second beggar stepped forward and with head held high he called out, 'The Devil is good.' The miser's friends were angered by his words. 'You speak a lie,' said the eldest and wisest among them, 'so you shall have nothing. Be gone!' They sent him away with naught but a foot up his backside and much cursing besides.

A third beggar came into the room and stood in front of the miser's family and friends, the beggar who you met at the start of my tale, a poor pauper who was not all he seemed. He looked at the great and the good gathered before him. He fixed all of them with a smiling eye and spoke, 'Ne'er a penny will you give me. You shall never ever give me a penny!' And so it was, none, not even the eldest and wisest among them could decide whether they should give the poor man a penny or no.

CHAPTER VII

THE COMMOTION TIME

OF THE FRIAR AND THE BUTCHER

Salt thy Flesh

On 19 August 1531, Thomas Bilney was burnt as a heretic at the Lollards Pit on the outskirts of Norwich. Bilney was executed for openly preaching against the veneration of saints, relics and pilgrimages. But this was the eve of the Protestant Reformation, which saw the gradual suppression of Catholic beliefs and the eventual separation from the Church in Rome.

Such was the change that in 1615, Thomas Tunstall was found hiding in Norwich and accused of being part of a 'Romish plot' to bring back the Catholic faith. He stated at his trial that he was 'a Benedictine monk by vow, but not act', but still was found guilty and hanged, drawn and quartered; his dismembered body was displayed on five of the city gates. The Counter-Reformation in Europe threatened the English Protestant Church and state and there was fear of Jesuit priests like Tunstall who were seen as fanatics and the terrorists of their day.

Such was the fear that they were hunted without mercy. In 1597, for example, Father John Gerard described how he was tortured in London:

> They took me to a big upright post, which held the roof of this huge underground chamber. Driven into the top of it were iron staples for supporting heavy weights. Then they put my wrists into iron gauntlets and ordered me to climb two or three wicker steps. My arms were lifted and an iron bar was passed through the rings of one gauntlet then through the staple and the rings of the second gauntlet. This done, they fastened the bar with a pin to prevent it slipping and then removing the wicker steps one by one from under my feet, they left me hanging by my hands and arms fastened above my head.[32]

These were frightening times when many did not know what to believe. Bilney, for example, while challenging many of the Catholic doctrines, did not deny the authority of the pope. The causes of the Reformation were complex, although for many it was about nothing more than greed and corruption in the Church. They focused their anger and dissatisfaction on the monastic orders of monks and friars who were thought to have rejected the Christian principles on which their orders were founded, while growing fat and wealthy on the backs of the laity.

That's why I have called this chapter The Commotion Time, a contemporary phrase, for it truly was a time of great fear, unheaval and religious intolerance, when many a monk, friar and nun were subject to much mockery in anti-clerical stories. They became exemplars of greed and popular figures of ridicule in England and found their way into many a Tudor tale. There are so many stories that they have spilt into other chapters of this book, although none were as greedy as the friar in this tale …

They used to say long ago that gluttony was a most grievous sin. To live to excess, to eat your fill and then eat some more was to go against the very word of God. Yet my story is about a wandering friar who had taken a vow of poverty and chastity, but was in truth a student of gluttony. He was supposed to follow God in heaven above, but instead only ever followed his desires on the earth below! He was as big in the middle as he was tall. He was a man of the Franciscan order, a grey friar as they were known, whose coarse tunic was large enough to cover three or perhaps even four of the leaner brothers of his order. The grey friar was a most corpulent fellow.

Well, the fat grey friar was on a journey with a leaner brother of his order, a man who only ate to live and was just a bit dull for all that. They had been travelling from here to there to somewhere else and now they were tired, hungry and footsore. And so it was, they decided to stop at the house of a butcher, there to beg a room for the night and perhaps a little food.

The butcher was not at home, but his wife was and she was a pious good woman. She knew in her heart that to be close to a friar was to be close to God in heaven above. She believed that there was 'perfection in poverty' and so the butcher's wife gladly let the fat and thin friars into her house. Picture the scene if you will: there was a large kitchen with a parlour on one side and a pantry on the other. At the far end of the kitchen was a roaring fire and next to the fireplace a door. Beyond the door were some stairs that curved up and around the chimney stack and led to one chamber above, the bedchamber of the butcher and his wife, although this night it would become the bedchamber of the two grey friars. For being a pious good woman who believed that to be close to a friar was to be close to God in heaven, there was no way the butcher's wife was about to let the two religious men sleep in her old cold barn.

The two were well pleased with their lodgings and the thin friar leapt upon the soft feather mattress. Soon he was asleep, dreaming of a life of love and light in heaven above. But the fat friar loitered long that night, for he had noticed that all that separated the chamber above from the kitchen below were thin wooden boards, badly joined and now he desired to hear that talk betwixt husband and wife and perhaps a little more! The fat grey friar knelt down, he set his ear to the boards and he listened and he listened and he listened.

It was now that the butcher returned home from a long day working at his trade and having no knowledge of the friars upstairs he greeted his wife and began to talk of the following day's business.

But before I go any further, you should know that the butcher was a complete and utterly different cut of meat to his wife. He had no time for religion and was more concerned with putting food on the table than with worrying about heaven or hell. He thought all religious men were greedy and lecherous and only cared about themselves. For some reason known only to himself the butcher had a particular dislike of Franciscan friars and such was his contempt, he called the two pigs in his sty outside 'his fat grey friars'. He thought that Franciscans and swine were much alike for, as he often said, both wallowed in their own desires! That's what the butcher thought, although his wife disagreed. Often she chided him for his blasphemous words, warning her husband that if he were not careful, then he would have the wrath of God upon him.

The butcher took little notice of his wife and this night he continued talking of the 'privy concernments of their household' meaning the most important jobs of the following day. 'Wife,' said the butcher, 'wife. On the morrow we must rise early, for I have noticed that one of our grey friars has grown very fat indeed. And so we shall slit their throats, salt their flesh and sell it at market.' The butcher laughed, but his wife did not. Nor did the fat friar upstairs, for having heard the butcher's words and believing them to tell of his own terrible doom, he leapt upon the bed and woke the leaner brother of his order. Sobbing loudly he told the thin friar all that he had heard from the kitchen below and now the other began to weep terrified tears. A devout man, he was not scared to die. It was just that he was not yet ready to leave this life!

But what could they do? They could not go down the stairs lest they pass through the kitchen where the butcher was already sharpening his biggest, meanest knife. 'We shall just have to leap from the window,' said the thin friar. 'We must risk the drop, for after all it can be no more terrible a doom than falling upon the butcher's meanest sharpest knife!' And so it was, the lean brother hung from the window frame and dropped to the ground. Being but a slight man he landed softly, but then he ran away. So much for being a brother! Seeing that he had been left to his fate, the fat friar leapt without prayer and without care from the window and landed with a crash and much swearing besides. His leg was sorely hurt and to make matters worse the butcher's dog had begun to bark. He could scarce walk, let alone run, and so the friar crawled to the only hiding place nearby – the butcher's pigsty, where he prayed for deliverance all night long.

But that night no succour came to the Franciscan and the following morning as the first cock crowed it found the butcher and his wife already up and dressed. She was cooking breakfast, while he put the finishing touches to his biggest, meanest knife. Having eaten his fill, the butcher left the house and called his wife to come with him. 'Hurry, wife,' he said, 'for it is time we were about slaughtering our fat grey friars.' He laughed as he always did, for the impious man loved to make sport of his wife's beliefs. Again she warned her husband that no good would come of his irreverent speech, but the butcher took no notice of his wife. Instead he marched up to his pigsty and called out, 'Come out, come out master grey friars, for it is my fixed intent this very morn to taste your chitterlings!'

But it was not a pig that crawled out of the sty that day to answer the butcher's call. Instead it was a real grey friar crawling on his hands and knees and calling out for mercy. 'Please don't slit my throat and salt my flesh,' he cried, 'and please don't sell my meat at market.' But the butcher did not reply, for the butcher was no longer there. If the friar was in fear of his life, the butcher was in no less, for it seemed that his wife had been right all along. It was a sign that he did indeed have the wrath of God upon him! And so it was the butcher ran away. Some say that he ran and he ran to the nearest monastery, where he became a monk and spent the rest of his life praying for his eternal soul. Others say that he ran and he ran until his feet were but bloody stumps and he fell over. But I like to think that he ran and he ran, and then he stopped. For having realised his mistake, he felt so foolish that he became a sailor, sailed the seven seas and was responsible for introducing the sausage to many a far off and distant land!

OF THE FRIARS AND THE MERCHANT

When the former mayor and merchant, Robert Jannys, died in 1530 he left money to the four orders of friars in Norwich in the hope that they would sing 'solem dirges', meaning prayers for his soul.[33] Friars lived off such payments and the charity of others and were traditionally 'mendicants' who travelled out into the world preaching and helping others in return for food and shelter.

But Jannys was writing on the eve of the Reformation and in just a few years such payments would cease. Such was the antagonism towards monks and friars by the early sixteenth century that many, like the butcher in the last tale, forgot that they provided care for the communities in which they lived. The dissolution of the monasteries, while welcomed by many, meant the loss of the traditional forms of charity that the religious had provided. But that's the beauty of stories and for every mocking tale, there is always a reply, even when it came to religion. After all, greed and vanity were not just the preserve of men of God: Robert Gybson, a self-made man who takes a fall elsewhere in this book, was a beer brewer from Norwich who built a conduit, a lead-lined pipe, to bring water from a well in St Lawrence parish 'for the ease of the common people'. This was 1575, post-Reformation, Protestant England and so I think it's fair to say that Gybson did not expect prayers in return for his generosity; rather it was to be a demonstration of his success, for as the carving on the stone wellhead stated to all who drank there, 'their ease was his cost, not small'.

And so to a tale where the religious are still celebrated and a greedy merchant is mocked ...

There were once two wandering friars. Not large greedy men like some religious folk you will read of in my book, just simple friars who travelled the land, spreading the Church's teachings and living off the kindness of others. For it was the rule of their order, the community to which they belonged, that they should live as the poorest in the land. As many believed long ago, to be poor was to be closer to God and most people long ago were happy to help a friar in need in the hope that they too might know salvation in heaven.

Well, it was Lent, a solemn time of holy observance, a time of atonement and self-denial, and the two friars had been on the road for many days, preaching at market crosses and helping all who they found in need. They had journeyed many miles this day and went to an inn to beg a meal from the landlord, who was well known for giving charity to monks, nuns and friars. But it was market day, the inn had been busy and the landlord had little to offer them. They had come too late, for he had just roasted the last of his fowl, a fat cockerel for an even fatter merchant to feast upon. The innkeeper, a man whose naivety was his only fault, suggested that the friars ask the merchant for a share of his dinner: 'For I feel certain,' said he, 'that a rich well-mannered gentleman such as he would gladly share some of his feast with godly men such as you.'

There sat the merchant, a well-fed, well-dressed man of worth, his fine fur-lined gown barely covering his ample belly, demonstrating to all that he was a wealthy man. But while he was big of body, the man of business had but a little heart, and human kindness was not a commodity in which he dealt. His mood was naturally foul and he had no wish to share his fowl with the two friars. Why should he a man made rich by his own hard work give to those who lived as common beggars?

The merchant eyed the cockerel greedily before turning to the friars and speaking of that which was on his mind. 'I would gladly share my chicken with you this day,' he said and he began to pull the succulent flesh from the bone as he continued, 'but tell me, brother friars is it not Lent?' 'It is,' the two mendicants replied. 'Then tell me this, good friars,' said the merchant, 'is not Lent a time for searching one's soul, a time of repentance when religious folk such as you remember how Jesus wandered in the wilderness and went for forty days without food?' 'It is,' the two mendicants replied. 'Then tell me, my fine fellows,' said the merchant, smiling at his own wit, 'is not Lent a time when friars such as you eat very little and no meat at all? Is that not the rule of your order?' 'Alas it is,' the two mendicants replied and with heavy hearts and grumbling stomachs they knew that they would not eat this day.

They could only watch as the merchant ripped into the cockerel's flesh, tearing at it with his hands and teeth, the meat scarce touching the sides as he greedily swallowed every morsel from the plate. Having finished his meal the rich man washed it down with some ale and rested a while before continuing his journey upon a fine well-built horse. A horse that had need to be well built for its load was not slight!

The two friars also continued on their way. They walked a good while and rested a while and they continued in such fashion until they came to a river that had burst its banks and there, sitting at the edge of the fast-flowing flood, was the merchant from the inn. He was well fed, but in poor humour, for his horse had lost a shoe and now he needed the two friars' help getting from one side of the river to the other. 'Alas,' he cried, 'what am I to do? For my horse is lame and my fine apparel would be ruined if I were to lead it across the river.' The merchant eyed the friars thoughtfully and spoke of that which was on his mind. 'Tell me brother friars, is it not a rule of your order that you help those in need?' 'It is,' the mendicants replied. 'Then answer me this, fine fellows,' said the merchant, smiling at his own wit, 'should not one of you carry me across the swollen stream on your back, while the other leads my horse?' 'Alas, we should,' the two mendicants replied and with a heavy heart the largest of the friars picked up the heavy merchant, while the other took hold of his horse and both waded into the cold deep waters.

But they had not gone more than halfway when both friars stopped, much to the annoyance of the rich merchant who asked them what was wrong? The largest friar with the largest burden winked at his brother before telling the merchant of that which was on his mind. 'Tell me, my friend,' said the friar to the merchant, 'have you been selling at the market this day?' 'I have,' the rich merchant replied. 'Then tell me this,' said the friar, 'have you made plenty of money this day?' 'I have that,' the impatient merchant replied. 'Then answer me this if you will,' said the friar to the merchant, 'do you carry the profits about you this day?' 'I do,' the boastful merchant replied and he lifted his gown so that both mendicants could see both pouch and purse bulging with coin. 'Then tell me this,' said the friar to the man of business clinging to his back, 'did you not know that it is the rule of our order that we must rely on the charity of others and carry no coin on our bodies?' And before the merchant could answer yay or nay the friar cast him into the cold icy water and he and his brother continued on their way. They may have had empty bellies, but both were full to the brim with wit, wisdom and also a good story to tell to any who would listen.

Of the Last Will and Testament

Sturdy christian Hound

In the Middle Ages, the Church had been used to living off the laity, the ordinary churchgoers who paid for prayers at their burials. They also paid tithes to their parish priest, or other monastic foundation, and payments for indulgences, meaning payments for the remission of sin, to say nothing of the monies to be made from pilgrimages. On one level, the medieval Church was a business like any other and a very profitable one at that. Hence the widespread criticism of the Catholic Church and antagonism that helped pave the way for Tudor Reformation.

After the Reformation, strictly speaking, such bequests could no longer speed a soul to heaven; good works could not ensure salvation. Such long-held beliefs were replaced with the doctrine of the elect, meaning that God had already elected the saved prior to them being born. That's not to say that the Protestant Church did not expect support from laity; they did. Tithes were still to be paid and the majority of people still left money to the Church in their wills. The Church had always known its rights and guarded them fiercely, taking the laity to court for unpaid tithes and bequests. As when Thomas Middletonne came before the consistory court for non-payment of thirty-three shillings and four pence bequeathed to Happisburgh church by a man called Bacon.

The continued greed of the Church is dealt with in this tale, but it's also a story about a dog. Of Tudor dogs I can say little. Many were loved by their owners, from the lapdogs of Tudor ladies to the mastiffs and greyhounds so prized by lordly hunters, but they were perhaps not so well regarded as they are today. Dogs were sometimes eaten during times of dearth and they were regularly killed along with other loose animals during times of plague. Many thought them brute beasts that had little value beyond hunting game and protecting their master's property. For as Shylock says in William Shakespeare's *Merchant of Venice*, 'Thou callest me a dog before thou hast cause. But since I am a dog, beware my fangs.' I'm not sure that the priest in this tale would have agreed with his sentiments.

There was once a priest who spent his days nurturing the poor of his parish, caring for their souls and helping them all as best he could. He was dedicated to his cause and spent little time thinking of himself but although he wouldn't admit it, the priest was a lonely man.

He did not know how unloved he felt until one day while out walking the bounds of his parish, he found a puppy abandoned by some cruel man. Nurturing was in his nature and so the priest took up the pup, took it home and set to raising it as a companion to keep him company on the cold winter nights.

Raise the mongrel he did and it grew into a fine hound that could better any other dog of the parish. Whether it be fetching a stick or fetching his cap when the wind blew fierce, the dog proved a great help to the priest and brought him much joy. The priest and his dog grew close, though many of his flock thought it strange, for this was a time when most called dogs 'curs' and thought them violent beasts who had little value beyond their bite.

At this time most dogs were bred for protection, or for hunting and to entertain the meaner sort, setting them against bears cruelly chained to a post. But not the priest's faithful hound, for he called him Sturdy and they spent every waking hour together, except when the priest was preaching in church! They lived happily for many years until it came to pass that Sturdy died. Whether it was the heat or the cold, or perhaps tainted meat, the priest did not know, but he was inconsolable. That his hound was lost to him, that there was no place for Sturdy in heaven and that they would never meet again was too much for the priest to bear.

And so it was, the priest decided to bury his dog in the churchyard, for as he told himself, it was only fitting that a good and intelligent companion as Sturdy have a proper burial. The dog was buried in consecrated ground and soon the story of a cur's Christian burial spread out across the land from village to town, from town to city and eventually from the city to the pages of this book. But before it reached you, the reader of this tale, it had already long ago found the ears of the bishop who had domain over the parish where the grieving priest dwelt.

Shocked by the cleric's blasphemous behaviour, the bishop sent for the sorrowful man so that he might explain himself, to tell all before God and his servants why he, the priest, had buried a soulless creature in consecrated ground. 'How dare you,' asked he, 'how dare you defile God's earth reserved for good Christians?' But the priest was ready for the bishop's outburst. He knew well enough that even devout men had their price. Like many long ago he was aware that for some, piety was a profession like any other and like any trade or craft long ago, its members demanded a wage!

'Why my good lord,' said the priest to his accuser, 'I have not defiled God's earth, for in truth my dog Sturdy was a good Christian soul.' But his words only served to anger the bishop more. So great was the prelate's wrath that if the Devil himself had sought to pay his compliments to the godly lord that day, he would have turned tail and run straight back to that fiery furnace from whence he had come. So vexed was the bishop that he ordered the village priest be put in prison, there to rot for his sacrilege.

'But my lord bishop,' begged the priest, 'my hound Sturdy was so devout in life and in death that he left many bequests in his will. So God-fearing was my dog that he willed coin to the poor of the parish and to the Church, including fifty gold crowns for you!' The priest took a purse from his belt and handed the gold coins over to the bishop, who took them gladly. Smiling now, he praised Sturdy's good sense and last testament and approved such a worthy animal be buried in the churchyard, for such a send off was befitting to any good Christian soul!

Well, where a simple parish priest got fifty gold crowns I cannot say, but since this is now your story, I think it only fair that you decide that for yourself.

OF FRIAR BACON'S CHOICE

he Reformation may have rid us of greedy monks and lusty friars, but it was much harder to change the ideas and beliefs of the common sort, the poorer people who had relied upon the Church for care and had sought solace in the simple idea that good works and a life well led meant even a poor person would find salvation in heaven.

Under the new Protestant faith, many were stripped of the ritual, colour and hope that the old Catholic Church had offered and felt increasingly vulnerable in a world that no longer seemed to have boundaries. A world where the radical Protestant William Morgan could be heard saying that 'religion was a matter of policy to keep men in awe and that adultery and fornication was no sin', and John Laws was burnt in Norwich castle ditches for 'being an obstinate blasphemer and pretended prophet who denied the divinity of Christ'.

The Reformation had unleashed all kinds of radical beliefs and religious non-conformism, which must have added to the woes of those who already lamented the loss of the Catholic faith. For not all monks and friars were seen in such a bad light and some were celebrated for their knowledge of the world about them. It is perhaps ironic that many of these godly men were the first scientists whose studies would in the fullness of time challenge the very notion of a divine creator in heaven. Although some suffered for their findings, including Roger Bacon, a thirteenth-century Franciscan friar who dabbled with optics and was imprisoned for his beliefs. So celebrated was Bacon that he became a hero of cheap print in the sixteenth century and remained a popular figure into the eighteenth. Some might think this strange in a time when many chose to mock the religious, but then again many harked back to simpler, less radical times. So enjoy a tale of a man whose wit and wisdom far outweighed his religious beliefs, a story that had something of the Shakespearian about it, reminiscent of his play about a foolish old ruler called Lear ...

There was once a rich farmer who lived in the West Country and went by the name of Bacon. He had one son whom he sent away to school in the hope that he might become wise and wealthy, in the hope that young Bacon might become a lawyer or a doctor who earned plenty of chinks and would care for the old farmer in his old age. Well, young Bacon took to his studies as a duck takes to water. He made a fine scholar and so quick was his wit that his contrary father worried that the boy was getting too big for the scholar's gown and cap that he wore. He took young Bacon out of school and set him to work upon the family farm.

But the boy missed his studies; he much preferred using his head to his hands. Young Bacon ran away to the University of Cambridge, until having learnt all there was to learn there, he sailed to France where he went to the University of Paris. When he had learnt all there was to learn at the University of Paris he sailed back to England and went to the University of Oxford.

He studied hard and when at last he had learnt all that he could there he became a friar, a wandering man of God. When not preaching to the masses, he continued his studies, pawing over dusty manuscripts, rediscovering long-lost knowledge from long, long ago, stirring pots of who knows what and staring up at the stars, while asking how and why. And so it was that Friar Bacon won great fame as a learned and wise man, skilled in the arts of science, alchemy and astronomy. He dabbled with early lenses and gunpowder and it was said that Bacon's head was so full of knowledge and wisdom that if you stood close to him and cocked your ear, then you could hear his skull creak and groan as it worked hard to keep all that wisdom inside!

Friar Bacon went on to perform many wondrous deeds. Once he crafted a fortune-telling head of brass and a gigantic wall that would surround England when her enemies attacked. Such was his renown that his wisdom was sought the length and breadth of the land and one day the king himself sent for the wise old man. He told Friar Bacon of a rich lord who had died leaving three sons, three sons who had few merits and many failings, or so their father had thought and so he could not decide who among them would inherit his titles and estates. And so the lord had willed it that it should be the son who had loved him the most.

Well, no sooner had the lord died than his three sons began to argue about who had loved their father most. Each argued that they 'had loved their father twice as much as the other two put together'. Such was their dispute that it reached the ears of the king, for all three were his wards. He listened patiently as all three claimed to have loved their father most. As all three argued that they 'had loved their father twice as much as the other two put together'. Each son was as convincing as the other, so that the king could not decide who among them should inherit his titles and estates. And so it was, he sent for wise Friar Bacon in the hope that he was as clever as others had often claimed. It would be up to the old man of God to judge who among them had truly loved their father most.

Bacon listened carefully as each of the three sons argued that they 'had loved their father twice as much as the other two put together'. Each son was as convincing as the other, so that even the old friar could not decide. And so it was he ordered that their father's corpse be fetched from its tomb and that the body should be lashed to a tree. He gave each of the three sons an arrow and held out a great yew bow. 'Take this bow,' said Friar Bacon, 'shoot your arrows into your dead father's body and the one that gets closest to the dead man's heart, he shall be the winner, he shall inherit his father's titles and estates.'

The eldest son snatched the bow from old man Bacon. He fitted the arrow, leant, aimed and shot. The arrow struck his father's body with a thump, but it did not hit the dead man's heart. The second son snatched the bow from the first. He fitted the arrow, leant, aimed and shot. The arrow struck his father's body with a thump, but it did not hit the dead man's heart. The third and youngest son took the bow from his brother. He fitted an arrow, leant and aimed, but now both boy and bow began to shiver and shake. A bead of sweat, or was it perhaps a tear, ran down the lad's face and he jerked the bow skyward, loosing the arrow so that it flew over field and meadow and disappeared into the woods beyond. 'I cannot do it,' he cried, 'I cannot shoot my own father,' thus proving it was he who loved his father most. Thus proving that he should inherit his father's titles and estates. Thus proving that Friar Bacon was the wisest man in the whole of England.

CHAPTER VIII

FACT OR FICTION, TRUTH OR LIES?

OF DRAKE THE WIZARD

In George Gifford's *Discourse of the Subtle Practices of Devils by Witches and Sorcerers* (1587) he described a witch as someone 'that worketh by the Devil, or by devilish curious arts, either hurting or healing, revealing things secret or foretelling things to come, which the Devil hath devised to entangle and snare men's sails withal damnation'.[34] The Devil was perceived as a real physical presence, the embodiment of evil, as were those who dealt with him. And yet, when in 1578 Ann Robson was accused of 'receiving idle rogues in her house and threatening some that if they will not spend their money in her house, she will make them dance naked by the use of her black cat', she was only threatened with a whipping if ever she did it again! Ann was clearly threatening witchcraft, but the court was more concerned with her harbouring idle men in her house. That's not to say that witchcraft and devilry were always taken so lightly, but in the sixteenth century paranoia over such things had not yet reached the hysterical heights it would during the religious and political turmoil of the mid-seventeenth century.

The Devil often appears in Tudor stories including the ones about Sir Francis Drake. Some attempts were made in cheap print to present real histories of heroes like Drake, for a more discerning reader, although clearly not in the stories below. Fantastical and strange tales were being told about the man and all aimed at a less discerning audience! His stories revolve around his almost magical abilities and I suspect that's because his rise to fame was meteoric, coming as it did in the wake of the Spanish Armada and its crushing defeat.

Such was Drake's fame that he became a major celebrity and in the months following the defeat of the Armada he toured the country. Drake heard tell of the skill of the Norwich Waits, the city's own musicians, and asked them to join him on his next voyage to Portugal. Five of the Waits agreed to go and the city spared no expense kitting them out for the voyage. The court records tell us that they were to have:

> VI [six] cloaks of stammel cloth made them ready before they go; and that a wagon shall be provided to carry them and their instruments, and that they shall have iiij li [four pounds] to buy them three new hautboys [a woodwind instrument] and one new treble recorder, and x li [ten pounds] to bear their charges; and pay Peter Spratt xs 3 d. [ten shillings and three pence] for a sack-but case.

This was a great honour for both the city and the musicians, although the joy was to be short-lived; it was an ill-fated voyage. Drake lost over forty ships and many a soldier and sailor died, including three of the five City Waits who joined the adventure. Their widows were granted a one-off payment of fifteen pounds and a pension of fifteen shillings per year.

Failure such as this may have damaged Drake's reputation at court, but not among the populace and the stories about him grew stranger still, for it was said that Drake, like Ann Robson, had done a deal with the Devil himself ...

Long ago on the south coast of England and in a time when gallant men wore small pointy beards and feathers in their caps, foreign sails were sighted on the horizon. Well, many an Englishman and many an Englishwoman fell into a panic, for this was a Spanish Armada, a great fleet of ships with an army on board, coming to return us to the Catholic faith and usurp the throne of England, to replace a fair queen with a foul king! But our ships were not ready to do battle with the great Spanish fleet. They were yet to weigh anchor, their sails were not set and their cannons were neither pricked, primed nor loaded.

Many an Englishman and many an Englishwoman fell to fretting, but there was one who did not and his name was Francis Drake. Instead our hero in the making finished his game of bowls upon Plymouth Hoe and then he sat down upon a rock. He took up a stick, took out his knife and set to whittling a twig while other sea captains looked on in despair, for our ships were not ready to do battle with the great Spanish fleet. They were yet to weigh anchor, their sails were not set and their cannons had not been pricked, primed or loaded. Yet still Drake continued whittling the stick until he had a great pile of shavings in front of him and now he stooped down and took up the whittled wood. He walked to the water's edge, cast them in and no sooner did the whittlings hit the waves then each and every one of them was transformed, remade as a warship. Each became an English man-of-war ready with their anchors weighed, sails set and with cannons pricked, primed and loaded. Drake's ships sailed out to meet the foreign fleet, sinking many a Spanish ship, while the rest of the Catholic Armada sailed home, never to darken our horizon again!

Well, I know what you are thinking, that's not how it was. The Spanish ships were decimated by great storms, a judgement from God perhaps, but this is not a story about Him in heaven, instead it is a tale of the Devil from hell! Such was Drake's fame and rise from obscurity that there was much talk of sorcery, that he was a wizard who had done a deal with Old Hob himself.

For at another time, a drought covered the land and the sun shone so fierce in the south of our fair country that water was scarce. Such was the heatwave that the goodwives of Plymouth complained that their wells had run dry and that they had not water enough to wash their clothes, nor to brew their ale. The talk of no ale caused a great tumult of the people. So great was the panic that many an Englishman and many an Englishwoman fell to fretting, but there was one who did not and his name was Francis Drake. Instead he leapt upon his horse and rode swiftly to Dartmoor where he searched all day until he found a spring of water flowing fast, cool and clear. Drake leant from his horse and whispered wondrous words, so that the spring reared up and followed close behind his horse, washing its hooves as Captain Drake galloped quickly back to Plymouth. And so it was that the wells of that fair town were filled, the goodwives' clothes were washed, ale flowed freely and already there was drunken talk of Drake's skill at the dark arts.

Such was his fame and such were his powers that Drake's reputation as a necromancer grew large and the tales of his adventures grew larger and stranger still. For once when he was sailing off the Spanish Main it was said that the wind suddenly dropped leaving his ships becalmed. The sea sat like a mirror, with not a ripple to be seen and all was quiet, save only for the murmuring of superstitious old sailors and their talk of Jonah, of God's judgement and of mutiny! They were knaves to a man and with black hearts they spoke of taking over the ships and of casting Captain Drake into the deep dark depths, but before they could do the devilish deed up sprang the Devil himself! They could tell straightaway that it was the Devil for his shoes were horny, his hose were hairy and the wicked horns on top of his head were only matched by the villainous look in his eye and his lawless laugh. 'Nah Ha, Nah Ha, Nah Ha, Ha, Ha, Ha, Ha!' What little courage Drake's men had, now it departed them. It ran away and so did they, hiding behind cannon and mast, in half-empty water barrels and between great coils of rope, while others scuttled below decks or threw themselves overboard, preferring to meet death in the deep dark depths rather than shake hands with the Devil himself.

All the English sailors fell to fretting; all that is save one, Francis Drake. Instead he bowed low to Old Hob, showing him all due honour that one gentleman should bestow upon another and so impressed was the Devil that he in turn bestowed two gifts upon the great sea captain: a spyglass and a drum. 'Beware,' said the Devil, 'for these are no ordinary favours I offer you this day. Both are magic!' He held the drum aloft, telling Drake that if ever he were becalmed again then all he need do is beat the drum softly and a gentle wind would blow to speed his ships on their way. 'But,' said the Devil himself, 'if ever you are attacked by pirates or by the Spanish, then all you need do is beat the drum loudly and a great storm with sink your enemy's ships!' Next, the Devil held up the spyglass, telling Drake that with such a tool as this he could see into the future. 'Whensoever you look through this glass,' said Old Hob, 'you will see other times and other places!'

Well, Drake gladly took the gifts from the Devil and with that his fate was sealed. The bargain was made, a life of magic in exchange for his eternal soul. And as you've already heard tell Drake used his powers for good. But it is unlikely that even the best of lives lived would impress the Devil himself and so what happened to Drake when this world was done with him I cannot say. Drake, however, had no mind for such things, for looking through his new spyglass he saw his true love Elizabeth. So long had he been away at sea, that Drake saw her weeping bitter tears thinking that her beloved was dead. He saw another wooing her, telling her to wait for Francis no more. Drake looked again and now he saw Elizabeth betrothed to the other man. There they stood in a church in Devon, the priest talking of her duty to her husband-to-be. And so it was that Drake ordered that a cannon be pricked, primed and loaded with powder and shot and that it be aimed directly into the sea. His men thought their captain mad, but all were afraid and so all followed his orders. They aimed the cannon into the waves and fired. The cannonball passed through water and rock, right through the centre of the earth and burst forth in the church where Elizabeth was to wed. The red-hot cannonball came to rest between Elizabeth and her husband-to-be, and such was the blast that many an Englishman and many an Englishwoman in the church that day fell to fretting, but there was one who did not and that was Elizabeth. Instead she looked upon the iron ball and spoke. 'This is Drake's shot,' said she. 'He is still alive, I cannot marry this day.'

Elizabeth waited for Drake and when after three years at sea he returned home they wed. Drake, they say, lived a long and happy life with Elizabeth and thought not of the hellish torments to come. And perhaps with good reason, for maybe he was able to outwit the Devil himself, just like the poor wife whose story is also set down in the book. There are many who say that he did escape hell and that like the fabled King Arthur before him, Drake slumbers in some dark place. There he sleeps, waiting for his magic drum to beat loudly. Only then will great storms lash our shores and Sir Frances Drake shall rise once more!

OF MERRY MASTER SKELTON

he boundary between fact and fiction, truth and lies, is often blurred and the merry jests about Robert Skelton demonstrate just that. Skelton found fame as an academic, poet and tutor to the young Henry VIII, but fell from grace and was imprisoned for a while by Thomas Wolsey. Later, as a priest in Diss, Norfolk, he caused even more scandal by secretly marrying his housekeeper and siring a child by her! It's not that hard to believe really since priests were always being accused of such things long ago. As when Richard Fox, the rector of Wortham in Suffolk, was called 'a naughty priest and a whoremonger'. There is also the case of John Norton, a priest, who was found guilty of 'keeping company with Betterys Skinner at unlawful times'. It was ordered that both John and Betterys 'shall ride in a cart about the market with papers (on their heads) for evil rule of long time used and so be tinked about the town with basins'. The 'tinking' of basins refers to the striking of pots and pans and general 'rough music' that accompanied such shaming punishments to ensure that their humiliation was complete.

Skelton, like Drake and other characters both fictional and real, drew earlier stories to him. Many of the jests attributed to him in *The Merry Tales Made by Master Skelton* (1567) had already been published elsewhere, including *The Parson of Kalenborowe* (around 1520). In most of these tales Skelton is a mischief-maker akin to a trickster, who gets the better of all that he meets. Yet there is a tale from another source that is also included below and in which Skelton, like Norton the priest, was also shamed ...

There was once a gentleman and Skelton was his name. His fame was great, but his credit was light. Some said he was a bit of a rascal, but others called him knave, rogue or worse. For although he was an educated man, a rector of the town of Diss and a poet laureate no less, he was a self-glorious sort, a contentious cleric who fell foul of many he met.

Once when on a journey he stopped at an inn and partook of salted meat and bread, but so salty was the flesh that he awoke in the night feeling parched and in need of ale. He called to the tapster to bring him some drink, but the servant of the inn heard him not. And so Skelton called to his host, but he was sound asleep and did not reply.

Such was Skelton's thirst that he thought he would burn and so he called out, 'Fire! Fire! Fire!' and now he heard the screams of other guests, and the hustle and bustle of the host and his servants as they ran from room to room making sure everyone was safe. Again Master Skelton cried out, 'Fire! Fire! Fire!' and the host, his wife the hostess, the tapster and many more besides burst into his room, all half naked and only half awake. 'Where?' asked the host, 'Where? Where is the fire? And Skelton pointed to this mouth. 'Here! Here! Here!' he replied, 'so fetch me some drink so that I might quench the flames in my mouth.' Ale was fetched, but I fear that Master Skelton was not made welcome at that particular inn again!

Skelton continued on his way, yet still he was a thirsty fellow and he stopped at a tavern where the wine was goodly and flowed freely for those who had coin enough to pay. He sat all day making merry in the tavern and so tasty was the wine and so good the company that he returned to the same establishment the following day. But the wine was not as fine as it had been the day before and Skelton feared that the vintner's wife had watered it down, but he could not prove it and it grieved him sorely.

And so it was that he sat down alone and did sigh and moan and lament his situation for all to hear and see. The vintner's wife came over to Master Skelton and asked the man, 'What ails you so?' Skelton replied, 'Alas that I shall never go to heaven for such a wrong I have done this day,' and now he begged the woman to promise that if he told her his secret that she would tell no other. She swore upon her soul that she would keep his counsel, for the vintner's wife was a gossip and a busybody of great renown, desperate to know why he despaired so much of God's mercy? 'Know this, goodwife,' said Skelton, 'this day I sent to you for wine to say Mass, but we have a law in our church that each priest must mix it with water in his chalice, his sacred cup to signify the pure blood of Christ. But I shall burn in hell for I forgot the water and only poured wine this day.' Skelton threw up his arms and wailed, 'Oh woe is me that I shall surely burn.' But the vintner's wife laughed loudly and smiled sweetly upon the poet and priest, 'Fear not, Master Skelton,' said she, 'be merry and know that you are saved, for by my faith I have mixed many gallons of water with the wine I sold this day.' Skelton's fears were realised and he cursed that woman for her evil brewing and great greed vowing never to buy from her again.

Skelton went home and continued with his base ways and ill behaviour. Such was his low fame that other clerics would have naught to do with him, including the Bishop of Norwich. And so it was that the wayward rector went to see the bishop at his palace, bringing him a present of two capons to sweeten his lord. But the bishop's palace was barred and Master Skelton was forced to crawl through gutter and sewer to get to his goal. He fought his way through foul filth and stench and entered the bishop's chamber, but still the old man would not receive him. 'My lord,' said Skelton, 'look here, for I have brought you two capons to feast upon with me.' But the bishop would not accept them. He called Skelton a knave, a lewd liver and a keeper of ill rule in his house, saying 'I will not dine with you, but I will keep the fowl for myself.' 'Fowl!' replied Skelton, 'how dare you call them fowl? These capons are no ordinary birds, they are the most special of gifts.' 'How so?' asked the bishop, fearing that he had made a mistake. 'Well,' Skelton replied, 'these two birds are so remarkable that both have names. The one is called Alpha, meaning the first, for it is the first fowl I have ever offered you. The other is called Omega, meaning the last, for it is the last gift you shall ever receive from me!' And Skelton turned his back upon his lord and left, proving himself worthy once more of his degrees from Oxford and Cambridge!

But know this: Master Skelton did not always get his own way, nor did he always have the last word. Like many of his age he could get above himself and as everyone knows the higher you climb, the longer the drop! For once a poor man came knocking at Skelton's door begging for alms and whatever other comfort the gentleman could provide. But the pauper was loathly to behold. His clothes were fusty, his flesh was foul and he did stink like an alehouse jakes. So black and dirty was the beggar that Master Skelton stepped back from him, seeking to shut the door upon the poor man, saying 'tarry here no longer man, for you look as though you have come from hell this day.' The poor beggar, seeing that Skelton would give him nothing but a tongue-lashing, replied: 'Why my lord, you speak the truth. I did come from hell, but was forced to leave. For alas,' he continued, 'there is no room for poor beggars such as me in hell, as it is kept only for gentlemen such as you!' And so it was the beggar left with an empty belly and for a while at least Master Skelton felt empty inside.

OF THE REWARD FOR LYING

As a storyteller I'm often asked if my stories are true and I say that there is a nugget of truth in all of them. Drake, after all, was a great sailor and Skelton a wayward priest. But the final story in this chapter is about a good king and I'm not sure if there has ever been such a thing! Some monarchs were of course better than others, but does that make them good? Was Queen Mary as bloody as they say and did her half-sister Elizabeth truly have the heart of a lion? Well, that depends on your point of view and your religious persuasion, whether you were a Catholic or a Protestant in those tumultuous times!

The story below is of a chivalrous medieval king, but one adapted in the sixteenth century. It promotes the ideal of kingship, of humility and strength, not the reality of paranoid Tudor court that was so often in crisis, weakened by infighting and rivalry and constant concern over providing an heir to the throne. So paranoid was the state that it worked hard to promote the monarchy in a positive light. Even Henry VIII appears in a chapbook tale of his own; a tale that was popular into the seventeenth century, in which he wanders the streets in disguise to find out what his subjects think of him, eventually rewarding a cobbler with a yearly pension for his honesty.[35]

The keyword here is humility, but Tudor monarchs, like their medieval predecessors, rarely rewarded honesty and fiercely guarded both their reputation and position. In 1578, Mathew Hammond, a wheelwright, was accused of 'seditious and slanderous words against the Queens Majesty'. He was fined one hundred pounds and because he couldn't pay he was put in pillory and his ears were cut off. But Hammond continued saying that 'the New Testament and the gospel of Christ were mere foolishness, a story of a man, a mere fable'. The Norwich authorities sent him to London where he was tried for blasphemy and sedition; he was found guilty and brought back to the city where he was burnt in the castle ditches. Hammond was a radical Protestant whose beliefs challenged the doctrines of the established church, but because Queen Elizabeth, like her father before her, was defender of the faith, any attack on religion was also an attack on her.

Not that her half-sister, Mary Tudor, and her court were any less oppressive. In 1554 Sir Thomas Wyatt and many of his supporters were executed for rebelling against her marriage to Philip of Spain, while in the same year Robert Gold was put in the pillory and he too had his ears cut off for publishing treasonable songs 'against the Queen's majesty'. In the light of such evidence you must make of this story what you will …

For this story we must leave fair England for a while at least and travel instead to far-off Italy, where there once lived a simple labouring man. He was a thresher and winnower of grain by profession, a lowly labourer with high-minded ideas. I cannot say how or why, but the grain winnower of Italy longed to be more than what he was. He wanted to give up the life of a labouring man, to lead instead a rich noble life in the service of a king.

The king he chose was Edward I of England, for the poor Italian had heard many a tale of his good humour and largesse towards those who served him well. And so the poor winnower boarded a ship and sailed to London and with no amount of effort on his part the Italian found his way to the great hall of the most royal of Edward's many palaces, where he now knelt before the king, offering himself up as a courtier; offering to do the old king's bidding.

But Edward ignored the plain and simple man, leaving him kneeling for the longest of times. And so it was the Italian winnower of grain decided to honour the king with words suited to his sovereign status. He called him, 'the Flower of Kingship', and compared the monarch to a noble rose, while all others were no better than worker bees attracted by his strength, beauty and just rewards. He talked of the king's great valour in battle and his wisdom that was 'equal to that of Solomon himself'.

The little Italian would have gone on with rustic rhetoric, his fine and gracious words, had not Edward leapt to his feet and knocked him off his knees, raining down many a punch upon the simple and somewhat confused man. The grain winnower crawled away to tend his wounds, and thought of the great journey he had made, the great hardships he had endured to meet, as he had been told, the most noble of lords and so he returned to the hall and cursed the king for his cruelty, calling him ungrateful and wicked. He said that the king was not high at all, but a lowly fellow who would return bad for good.

The little Italian would have continued with his mocking insults, had not Edward leapt once more to his feet so that the simple man ducked, fearing that he had gone too far. Many in the king's court gasped and even wailed and winced at the poor winnower's wild words. But though Edward laid his hands upon the poor man again, it was to embrace him this time. The king called to his servants to fetch the finest of his many robes, which he placed upon the Italian winnower's shoulders, a reward for honest words, well spoken and ample compensation for the beating he had endured.

The little Italian left London and returned to Italy with a fair gown and much money besides. He travelled to many an Italian court and told a multitude of Italian lords the very story that I have just told you. Everyone he told, from noble knight to gracious lady, enjoyed hearing tell of the simple winnower's adventures in Edward's court and he was paid handsomely for the tale, for in doing so all his lordly listeners lay claim to Edward's humility, taking it for their own.

Alas, though, we all know these are just words set down in a simple book of folk tales and while I think many of the stories told here reflect the ideas and beliefs of Tudor times, I am less certain about this one. That is why I have made it the last tale in my book, to remind us all that actions speak louder than words!

Notes

1. J. Jewel, *A Homily Against Disobedience and Willful Rebellion* (1571), part 2.
2. E. Tilney, *The Flower of Friendship: A Brief and Pleasant Discourse of Duties in Marriage* (1568), p. 6.
3. Tilney, p. 12.
4. Tilney, pp. 29, 31.
5. W. Shakespeare, *The Comedy of Errors* (*c*.1594) act 2, sc. 2.
6. B. Cozens-Hardy and E.A. Kent, *The Mayors of Norwich, 1403–1835* (1938), p. 68.
7. Cited in M. Spufford, *Small Books and Pleasant Histories, Popular Fiction and its Readership in Seventeenth-Century England* (1981), p. 245.
8. W. Shakespeare, *Henry VI, Part III* (*c*.1591) act 5, sc. 6.
9. T. Johnson, *Of the Generation of Man*, cited in T. Laquer, *Making Sex: Body and Gender from the Greeks to Freud* (1990), p. 162.
10. W. Shakespeare, *Love's Labour's Lost* (*c*.1595) act 2, sc. 1.
11. *The Witty Maid of the West*, in W.G. Day, *The Pepys Ballads* (1987), p. 17.
12. P. Stubbs, *The Anatomie of Abuses in England* (1583), p. 31.
13. *Of Whoredom and Uncleaness*, in J. Chandos, *In God's Name, Examples of Preaching In England, 1534–1662* (1971), pp. 59–60.
14. W. Vaughn, *Approved Directions for Health* (1600), cited in A. Fletcher, *Gender and Subordination in England, 1500–1800* (1995) p. 76. Also T. Logan, *The Haven of Health* (1596), cited in Fletcher, p. 45.
15. W. Shakespeare, *The Two Gentlemen of Verona* (*c*.1589) act 1, sc.1.
16. 'The Orders for the Poor' (1571) in R.H. Tawney and E. Powers, *Tudor Economic Documents, Vol. 2* (1951), p. 316.
17. For further detail on the census see J. Pound, *Tudor and Stuart Norwich* (1988), pp. 31–45.
18. Spufford, p. 51.
19. T. Harman, *A Caveat or Warning for Common Cursetors* (1566), cited in Tawney and Powers, *Vol. 3*, pp. 407–8.
20. Letter cited in Tawney and Powers, *Vol. 2*, pp. 337–8.
21. 'An Act for the Punishment of Vagabonds, and for Relief of the Poor and Impotent' (1572), cited in Tawney and Powers, *Vol. 2*, p. 328.

22. W. Shakespeare, *Measure for Measure* (c.1603) act 5, sc.1.
23. W. Harrison, *Description of England* (1587), cited in A.H. Dodd, *Life in Elizabethan England* (1975), p. 151.
24. For further detail about the plague, see for example F. Meeres, *A History of Norwich* (1998), pp. 53–4.
25. For Tudor wills see for example Cozens-Hardy and Kent, pp. 372–89.
26. *Of Beggars*, cited in Tawney and Powers, *Vol. 3*, pp. 405–6.
27. 'The Orders for the Poor' (1571), cited in Tawney and Powers, *Vol. 2*, p. 316.
28. G.R. Batho, *The Household Papers of Henry Percy, Ninth Earl of Northumberland, 1564–1632* (1962), p. 64. A. Hassell Smith, *The Papers of Nathaniel Bacon of Stiffkey* (1983), *Vol. 2*, p. 75.
29. 'An Act for Punnishment of Rogues, Vagabonds and Sturdy Beggars' (1597), cited in Tawney and Powers, *Vol. 2*, pp. 354–5.
30. 'The Decaye of England Only by the Great Multitude of Shepe' (1550–53) cited in Tawney and Powers, *Vol. 3*, pp. 51–2.
31. For a full transcript of Robert Janny's will see N.P. Tanner, *Popular Religion in Norwich with Special Reference to the Evidence of Wills, 1370–1532* (1963), pp. 397–402.
32. J. Gerard, *Autobiography* (1609), cited in Dodd, p. 164.
33. For Tudor wills see for example Cozens-Hardy and Kent, pp. 372–89.
34. G. Gifford, *Discourse of the Subtle Practices of Devils by Witches and Sorcerers* (1587), cited in Dodd, p. 171.
35. Cited in Spufford, p. 222.

GLOSSARY

Alchemy – a forerunner to modern chemistry, but steeped in magic
Alewife – a female tavern keeper
Bawd – a brothelkeeper
Beguiler – someone who uses charm to deceive another
Benedictions – religious blessings, often part of a church service
Blockhead – a stupid person
Bridewell – house of correction for idle persons and vagrants
Cabinet – a private room
Cage – a metal cage that hung near the market for shaming petty offenders
Chapman – an itinerant seller of goods, such as chapbooks
Chinks – slang term for coin
Chitterlings – the cooked small intestines of pig
Churl – a rude or mean spirited person
Clot-brain – an idiot
Coney – a rabbit or gullible person
Coney-catcher – a con man who preyed upon the gullible
Corpulent – someone who is fat
Cozenage – to deceive
Cuckold – a husband whose wife has cheated on him
Cutpurse – a thief who cuts people's purses from their belts
Distaff – a staff used to hold wool prior to spinning it into thread
Dolt – a fool
Doublet – a tight-fitting buttoned jacket popular from the fourteenth to seventeenth centuries
Dullard – a slow stupid person

Filberts – alternative name for a hazelnut

Filch – to steal something of small value

Firmament – the sky or heavens

Flibbertigibbet – a frivolous, excitable person, most often used to describe a female

Galled – annoyed

Giglet – a playful girl

Gleaned – collecting leftover crops from harvested fields

Gluttony – greed

Goodwife – female head of a household

Haunter of alehouses – someone always out drinking

Hogshead of wine – a large cask and measure of wine

Humours – the four main fluids of the body, believed to govern a person's health

Irked – annoyed

Japed – slang term for sexual intercourse

Knave – a dishonest person

Lecherous – excessive sexual desire

Leech – slang term for a doctor

Lewd – rude and/or bad behaviour

Lusty – healthy and strong

Mendicant – someone from a religious order who relied solely on charity

Miser – someone who hoards money

Mountebank – a con man

Naked shirt – a semi-naked person

Ninny-Hammer – a fool

Palliasse – a straw mattress

Pauper – a very poor person

Pedlar – an itinerant seller of goods

Pestilence – any epidemic disease, most commonly used to refer to bubonic plague

Pilgrimage – a journey to a shrine where saints bones and other relics were kept

Pillory – a device for locking a wrongdoer's head and arms in place

Pious – someone who is religious

Pisspot – a chamber pot

Poorly wrought – badly made

Pox – a viral disease, the symptoms of which include pus-filled pimples

Reformation – change from the Catholic to Protestant faith in sixteenth-century Europe

Relic – the remains of a saint, bones etc., to which magical powers were often attributed

Rogue – a dishonest person

Rough music – raucous music often accompanying ritual and punishments

Ruff – an elaborate collar worn by the rich

Sarcenet – a soft silk used for lining clothes

Scold – a nagging, noisy woman

Sickle – a hand-held semi-circular bladed tool for cutting crops

Sluggard – a lazy person

Stocks – a device for locking a wrongdoer's legs in place

Sweating sickness – a highly virulent disease of the fifteenth and sixteenth centuries

Tabor – a small drum

Thither and yon – archaic phrase meaning here, there and everywhere

Tithes – one tenth of all produce paid to the Church

Unwiped, tardy gaited, bed-presser – a dirty, slow and lazy person

Vagabond – a dishonest and/or homeless person

Vagrant – a homeless person

Vexed – angry

Villain – a criminal

Wall Eye – someone with a lazy eye

Ward – someone placed under the legal guardianship of another

Whore – a sexually promiscuous woman

Whoremonger – a sexually promiscuous man

Wittol – a man who is complicit in his wife's adultery

BIBLIOGRAPHY

UNPRINTED PRIMARY SOURCES

Norfolk Record Office:
Consistory Court Deposition Books, NRO/NCR/DEP/31, 1600–01
Proceedings of the Mayor's Court, NRO/NCR/16A/13, 1595–1603

PRINTED PRIMARY SOURCES

Batho, G.R., *The Household Papers of Henry Percy, Ninth Earl of Northumberland, 1564–1632* (Camden Third Series, 1962)

Chandos, J., *In God's Name, Examples of Preaching in England, 1534–1662* (The Bobbs-Merrill Company, 1971)

Cozens-Hardy, B. (ed.), *Norwich Consistory Court Depositions, 1499–1512 & 1518–1530* (Norfolk Record Society, 1938)

Cozens-Hardy, B. and Kent, E.A., *The Mayors of Norwich, 1403–1835* (Jarrold & Sons, 1938)

Day, W.G., *The Pepys Ballads* (DS Brewer, 1987)

Dodd, A.H., *Life in Elizabethan England* (Putnam, 1975)

Galloway, D., *Records of Early English Drama: Norwich 1540–1642* (University of Toronto Press, 1984)

Hassell Smith, A., *The Papers of Nathaniel Bacon of Stiffkey, Volume II, 1578–1585* (University of East Anglia, 1983)

Hudson, W. and Tingey, J.C., *The Records of the City of Norwich* (Jarrold & Sons, 1906)

Logan, T., *The Haven of Health* (1596)

Rye, W. (ed.), *Depositions taken before the Mayor and Aldermen of Norwich, 1549–1567: Extracts from the Court Books of the City of Norwich 1666–1688* (Norfolk & Norwich Archaeological Society, 1905)

Stubbs, P., *The Anatomie of Abuses in England* (1583)

Tanner, N.P., *Popular Religion in Norwich with Special Reference to Wills, 1370–1532* (University of Oxford D. Phil, 1973)

Tawney, R.H. and Powers, E., *Tudor Economic Documents, 3 Volumes* (Longmans, Green & Co, 1951)

Tilney, E., *The Flower of Friendship: A Brief and Pleasant Discourse of Duties in Marriage* (1568)

Vaughan, W., *Approved Directions for Health* (1600)

SECONDARY SOURCES

Ashton, J., *Chapbooks of the Eighteenth Century* (Skoob Books, 1991)

Briggs, K., *A Dictionary of British Folk Tales*, 4 Vols (Routledge & Kegan Paul, 1970–71)

Fletcher, A., *Gender and Subordination in England, 1500–1800* (Yale University Press, 1995)

Hellman, R. and O'Gorman, R., *Fabliaux, Ribald Tales from the Old French* (Thomas Y. Crowell, 1963)

Keen M., *The Outlaws of Medieval England* (Routledge & Kegan Paul, 1977)

Klaf, F.S. and Hurwood, B.J., (eds), *A Hundred Merry Tales: The First Version of the Collection of Lusty Pre Elizabethan Tales, Originally published in 1525 sometimes called 'The Shakespeare Jest Book'* (Citadel Press, 1964)

Krapf, N. (ed.), *Beneath the Cherry Sapling, Legends from Franconia* (Fordham University Press, 1988)

Laquer, T., *Making Sex: Body and Gender from the Greeks to Freud* (Harvard University Press, 1990)

Lippencott, H.F. (ed.), *Merry Passages and Jests: A Manuscript Jestbook of Sir Nicolas Le Strange, 1603–1655* (Elizabethan and Renaissance Studies, 1974)

Meeres, F., *A History of Norwich* (Phillimore, 1998)

Ohlgren, T.H. (ed.), *A Book of Medieval Outlaws, Ten Tales in Modern English* (Sutton Publishing, 1998)

Painter, W. (ed.), *The Palace of Pleasure, Elizabethan Versions of Italian and French Novels*, 3 Vols (University Press of the Pacific, 2002)

Pound, J., *Tudor and Stuart Norwich* (Phillimore, 1988)

Robbins, R.H. and Dobkin, A. (eds), *A Hundred Tales* (New York, 1960)

Scott, A.F., *Everyone a Witness: The Tudor Age* (Purnell Book Service, 1975)

Shah, I., *World Tales* (Octagon Press, 1991)

Spufford, M., *Small Books and Pleasant Histories, Popular Fiction and its Readership in Seventeenth-Century England* (Cambridge University Press, 1981)

Storer, E. (ed.), *Il Novellino, The Hundred Old Tales* (Headley Brothers, 1917)

Swan, C. and Hooper, W. (eds), *Gesta Romanorum, Or Entertaining Moral Stories* (Dover Publications, 1959)

Zall, P.M. (ed.), *A Hundred Merry Tales, and Other Jestbooks of the Fifteenth and Sixteenth Centuries* (University of Nebraska, 1963)